End of days in Bible Cides

Matityahu Glazerson

Published by Kings Judaica, 2024.

While every precaution has been taken in the preparation of this book, the publisher assumes no responsibility for errors or omissions, or for damages resulting from the use of the information contained herein.

END OF DAYS IN BIBLE CIDES

First edition. February 18, 2024.

Copyright © 2024 Matityahu Glazerson.

ISBN: 979-8224891528

Written by Matityahu Glazerson.

"END OF DAYS IN BIBLE CODE"
Enlarged edition
The Splendor of Jewish Wisdom -
"KABBALAH AND SCIENCE"
MATITYAHU GLAZERSON

MATITYAHU GLAZERSON

PREFACE

The book, "The End of Days in bible", introduces various tables relating different topics. Some of the tables were found by the author and Professor Eliyahu Rips of the Hebrew University of Jerusalem, including some with Professor Robert Haralick from the City University of New York" and Doctor Alexander Rotenberg.

Alexander Rotenberg received his Ph.D degree in mathematics in the field of Probability Theory and Dynamical Systems in 1973 at the Moscow State University. After his aliyah to Israel in 1990, Dr. Rotenberg became familiar with Torah codes.

Many tables shown in the book are also from other scientists, as is mentioned in the book. In the book, the author presents the ELS, Equal Letters Skip phenomenon, with the explanation of Professor Robert Haralick.

The author also brings the words of leading Rabbis regarding the importance if this subject being a convincing proof that the Torah is from Heaven.

A large section of the book explains the connection of Torah Codes to the fiftieth gate of understanding, which, according to Kabbalistic tradition, will be revealed by the coming of the Messiah. So too, the author elaborates on the connection of the Torah Codes and the Hidden Light.

The Author wants to thank very much to Roseanne Barr for her great contribution for this book.

To Mrs kim Stulman who went over the material and added very important remarks to the book.

INTRUDUCTION

The publication of the scientific findings of the 'Torah Codes', has stirred society toits foundation, since its computerized conception.

Many contemporary works have been written about the Torah Codes from various viewpoints. These works deal extensively with the meaning and methodology of **ELS** (Equidistant Letter Sequence, or Equal Letter Skip), which define Torah Codes as a (repeatable) science.

Until this point, many have not known that one of the most influential scientists in history, Sir **Isaac** Newton[1],was so ultimately convinced of the existence of Torah codes,that he learned Hebrew and spent half his lifetime trying to find them. However, no mathematical theory applied by him worked.

Professor Eliyahu Rips[2] succeeded only because he had the technology that Newton did not. **The hidden text of the Torah was encoded with a time-lock.**

No human eye could fully fathom or decipher the hidden encoding within the plain text. The full discovery of the Torah Codes had to wait until the computer was invented.

Newton would spend much of his life seeking and revealing what could be considered a Bible Code[1]. He placed a great deal of emphasis upon the interpretation of the Book of Revelation[2], writing generously upon this book and authoring several manuscripts detailing his interpretations.

Unlike a prophet[3] in the true sense of the word, Newton relied upon existing Scripture to prophesy for him, believing his interpretations would set the record straight in the face of what he considered to be "so little understood". In 1754, 27 years after his death, Isaac Newton's treatise, *An Historical Account of Two Notable Corruptions of Scripture*[4] would be published, and though it does not argue any prophetic meaning, it does exemplify what Newton considered to be just one popular misunderstanding of Scripture.

Although Newton's approach to these studies could not be considered a scientific approach, he did write as if his findings were the result of evidence-based research.

1.   https://en.wikipedia.org/wiki/Bible_Code

2.   https://en.wikipedia.org/wiki/Book_of_Revelation

3.   https://en.wikipedia.org/wiki/Prophet

4.   *https://en.wikipedia.org/wiki/An_Historical_Account_of_Two_Notable_Corruptions_of_Scripture*

The Post Newton Era

Today, one of the most outstanding contemporary works regarding the subject of Torah Codes is authored by **Doron Witztum** in his book, **"'Tzofen Bereshit"-The Code of Genesis'**, in which the author expands on the methodology of ELS (Equal Letters Skip). He also takes on the task to answer all its critics and opponents.

A large portion of the materials presented in this book may be quite difficult for the average reader, who is not proficient in mathematics and statistics, to comprehend.

Nevertheless, a contemplation of the charts presented in this book, will reveal a wonderful and profound phenomenon that can be observed from versatile view points:

A. By its statistical significance, which will be further expounded in the book.
B. The encoded findings fit, strikingly, with the actual content of the verses, and where they were found.

In the introduction of the book,'**Tzofen Bereshit** -The Code of Genesis,'Witzum cites the opinions of various scientists regarding the existence and reality of ELS Torah Codes, which includes the opinion of the renowned Mathematician: Professor **Yisrael Aumann**, 2005 recipient of the Nobel Memorial Prize in Economic Sciences (The Sveriges Riksbank Prize in Economic Sciences in Memory of Alfred Nobel).And member of the **American National Academy of Sciences.**

Professor Aumann states:

"If the discovery of the Torah Codes is correct, it is the greatest discovery in the 300 years history of scientific research."

Statistician **Professor Persi Diaconis**, a co-member of the **American National Academy of Sciences**, co-signed the following declaration:

'We concur that if this research is verified, it is of broad scientific interest and it has important consequences for the way in which we think about our physical world. This is not merely a matter of bible studies.'

Professor Tzvi Atzmon adds,

"If this phenomen is proven true, it will bring about a major revolution that will overshadow the Copernican Revolution."

He goes on to state, "If there is substance to this claim, then the foundation of human thought and man's understanding will be shaken."

In his book,'Tzofen Bereshit- The Code of Genesis', Doron Witzum expounds that most of the Torah Codes deal with matters that are 'Kabbalistic' in nature. For this reason, he turned to a contemporary Torah Scholar of whom he writes:

"Besides possessing broad knowledge of the Kabbalah, he knows how to analyze the deepest of this wisdom."

Showing him examples of his own findings, Witzum describes their wide-ranging discussion on the topic.

When Witzum asked the Kabbalist if these findings surprised him, he replied,

"From the theoretical viewpoint it is not a new concept, since our early Sages had already stated that there is nothing that is not allued to in the Torah".

Nevertheless, the Kabbalist acknowledged that these findings are exciting, since knowing about them in theory is one thing, but seeing them in front of our eyes is something else!

Doron Witzum then went ahead and told the Kabbalist that he encountered a strange reaction to his research from several Torah observant scientists.

They said that the research made them uncomfortable, not from a scientific standpoint, but from a religious one.

For example, one well known physicist could not tolerate the idea that the name **'Franz Joseph'** is encoded within the Torah.

The Kabbalist was amazed to hear this. He emphasized that **"When the Sages informed us that everything is alluded to in the Torah, they really meant everything".**

The Kabbalist mentioned that,on this subject, the Jewish Scholar, **The Vilna Gaon**[3], explained in his commentary(to **Sifra DiTzniuta,** which is a part of the Zohar[4]), that this statement of the Sages is meant to include even the most minute detail of the environment. He goes on to tell Witzum, "I think even Franz Joseph is included in this category."

The Kabbalist was primarily amazed at those scientists that dare to declare based on an *apriory* consideration on what is fit or not fit to be encoded in the Torah.

Did they write the Torah? he asked rhetorically, Is the Torah bound by their way of thinking? This is nothing more than prejudice!"

Witzum goes on to relate in his book that he inquired further of him, Can one really expect to find every subject in the hidden text?"

The Kabbalist, in turn, replied that **"in fact, everything is alluded to in the Torah,** and referred to a work by **Rabbi Moshe Cordovero**[5].

The book **'Pardess Rimonim'** lists numerous dissecting methods by which one can reach a level of understanding of new information, which was formerly hidden within the Torah text. This, therefore, allows one to interpretallussions given by the Torah.

To do so, not only the method of Equidistant Letters Sequence is used, but sometimes a combination of two or more methods are required to extract hidden information from the Torah[6].

Hence, according to the Kabbalist, the picture is complicated. He is of the opinion that what Witzum calls a "hidden text"is only one part - probably a small part - of the whole subject.

Finally, Witzum presented his main question to the Kabbalist Rabbi, in effort to receive a clear answer: "Is it, in fact, possible to decipher what I call a hidden text?"

The Kabbalist Rabbi looked at him in surprise. He replied in a gentle tone, which contained rebuke.

He had thought, he told him, that he had come to him after having studied the words of the **Ramak,** (Acronym for Moses Cordovero).

However, he now informed him, that according to the Ramak, our generation does not have the power to achieve knowledge of how to read the hidden text.

Witzum relates that at the end of their conversation, the Kabbalist remarked that the **"Professor's research has great value, in that it removes one of the barriers separating us from recognizing the truth".**

Merely proving the existence of the hidden text–and more so proving that it contains information which accurately describes future events, constitutes a wonderful revelation about the nature of truth.

When Witzum asked the Kabbalist whether he should continue his research on ELS Torah Codes, he answered without hesitation.

"If the Professor saw a need for further proofs for the existence of the hidden text, he should carry out his project to completion."

Vital Contributions to the Subject of ELS

A vital contribution to the subjet of ELS is the book, *And All This Is Truth*! - וזהכל אמת'by **Doctor Alexander Rotenberg.**

In his book Doctor Rotenberg presents ELS Codes of words in the Torah which coincide with the exegetical[7] and Kabbalistic teachings of the Sages.

Doctor Rotenberg also approached Jewish Scholars/Rabbis and showed them his body of work.

The Rabbis were excited by his discoveries because it allows one to strengthen their faith in the Divine origin of the Torah. They enthusiastically gave him their approbation for his book.

One of these approbations was given by Chief **Rabbi Chaim Pinchas Scheinberg** of Kiryath Mattersdorf (Community of Mattersdorf), who is also the Head of 'Yeshivas Torah Ohr- Jerusalem'.

Rabbi Scheinberg describes in his approbation that even though,for reasons known to him, he usually does not grant approbations for books, nevertheless, he gives his approbation to this body of work of ELS Torah Codes, because it will, as he states, 'Magnify the Torah, and glorify it'.

Rabbi Nechemia Zalman Goldberg,a halakhic[8] authority and **"Chief Justice of the Rabbincal High Court in Jerusalem"**, Israel and Head of the Kollel[9] 'Da'at Moshe Sadigura', writes in his approbation:

'"The materials in this book arouse tremendous excitement and compel the reader to acknowledge that everything in our Torah is true."'

Rabbi Yehuda Salman, Rabbi of the Haredim Community in Ramat Elchanan, Bnei Brak, and a member of the Bnei Brak Torah Court, writes in his approbation:

"The work "And is Truth!"By Doctor Alexander Rotenberg contains Wonderdul things that open up the heart and enlighten the eyes."'

The Gaon[10] Rabbi **Shlomo Fisher**, Head of the 'Itri Yeshivah – Jerusalem'was asked whether it is correct and desirable to occupy oneself with the study of Torah Codes.

His written reply received the concurrence of the Gaon Rabbi Shlomo Zalman Auerbach[11]. Rabbi Fisher writes, The Equidistant Letters Sequence Codes (ELS) strengthen and enhance the honor of the Torah.'

Rabbi Fisher compares it to the Torah, which in its narration and teachings, singles out specific anatomical features in animal species such as:

That of the camel, hare, rabbit, pig and fish (singling out features such as the scales and fins, among all fish.)

The Torah describes these anatomical features in detail. The Sages tell us (in Chulin 66b) that the reason for mentioning all these scientific and anatomical details is to 'Magnify the Torah and glorify it.' (Isaiah 42:22)

As Rabbi Fisher continues, **'"On the contrary, it** (the occupation with Torah Codes) **is a great Mitzvah**[12] **and in every generation there were Torah Sages who were experts in refuting apostates.'**

Rabbi Fisher continues, **'The Rabbis occupied themselves with proving the truthfulness of the holy Torah in ways that were understandable to their contemporaries.'**

This is so well known, say the Jewish Teachings,'no proof is needed'. Going to the Tractate[13] (Chullin 66b[14]) which asks rhetorically, 'Was Moses a trapper or a hunter?

[I.e. how did Moses know the names and features of all the many animals, birds, fish and insects mentioned and described in the Torah?]

This is the answer, say the Jewish Teachings, to those who claim that the Torah is not of Divine Origin. This is so well known that no proof is needed.

The contemporaries who research Torah Codes are G-d fearing and Torah observant people.They regard their research into the Torah Codes and their meanings as a means to strengthen their faith in the Divine origin of the Torah.

In fact their discoveries give them sublime pleasure, akin to the study of the Talmud.[15]

On the other hand there are unfortunately those who do not delve deeply into the significance of the Torah Codes, but instead regard them as a meaningless word game.

They, unfortunately, do not approach its study from an objective point of view and therefore fail to allow themselves to give its study the proper respect.

Rabbi Shlomo Fisher alludes to this group in a later section of his letter:

'**Certainly, those who occupy themselves with** [The Torah Codes] **are performing a great Mitvah (good deed) – with the condition that they are properly qualified in scientific knowledge.**

"Moreover, all those who occupy themselves with this in a spirit of faithfulness to the Torah will be blessed by heaven with all the blessings due to those who bring merit to the public and bring back the distant to Torah and the commandments.

G-d forbids that they should slacken in this, even by considerable piety and excessive righteousness.

For those who consider it more pious to refrain from such studies do not speak with true knowledge and would do better to remain silent.'

About the Authors of this Book

Robert Haralick holds a distinguished professorship position in Computer Science at the City University of New York. His area of research is pattern recognition,image processing, image analysis, computer vision, anddata mining.

He has published over 550 archival articles, book chapters, and conference papers in the scientific literature.

He is a previous president of the International Association for Pattern Recognition, is a Fellow of the Institute for Electrical and Electronic Engineers and aFellow of the International Association for Pattern Recognition.

Since 1990, he has been listed in every edition of Who's who in America.ProfessorHaralick first learned about Torah Codes in1992.Soon after; he met Rabbi Glazerson in one of those chance but no-coincidence meetings in Jerusalem.

In 1995, Professor Haralick and Rabbi Glazerson authored the book **'Torah Codes and Israel Today'**. This is the firstbook in which the remarkable connection between theTorah verses and the content of the Torah code table was explored.

In 1997, Professor Haralick began to seriouslystudy the statistical properties of the Torah Codes. Theappendix contains a technical description of some recentTorah code experiments that Professor Haralick completed.

These experiments provide solid statistical evidence for theexistence of Torah Codes and demolish the critic's argumentsthat codes with similar statistical properties can befound in any book.

Rabbi Glazerson is an internationally known lecturerand teacher. He has taught in Yeshivah Ohr Samayach inJerusalem and at NeveiYerushalayim, a girl's seminary in

Jerusalem.

He was a Rabbi at Yeshivah Torat Emet in Johannesburg, South Africa. He has been involved in bringing many Jewish youngsters back to their Jewish roots.

He has authored 25 books in Hebrew, most of which have been translated into Russian, French, and English. Forfifteen years, Rabbi Glazerson wrote a weekly column for'Yom Hashishi' in which he related words associated withcurrent events to other Hebrew words having the samegematria.

It is by way of gematria that Rabbi Glazerson teaches Torah. After Rabbi Glazerson and Professor Haralick began to work on Torah codes, Rabbi Glazerson began teaching Torah through Torah codes as well as gematria. Rabbi Glazerson is also a musician and composer.

He composed a tune to Shalom Aleichem that has become, even in his day, so popular a tune that peoplealready regard it as a folk tune.

CHAPTER ONE

WHAT IS ELS -"EQUAL LETTERS SEQUENCE?"

In this part of the present work we shall focus on the subject of the **equal-letter-skip codes**, explaining how they are revealed in the Torah, and providing meaningful and important examples.

What is an Equal-Letter-Skip?

An equal-letter-skip Torah code is a significant word or significant group of words found at equal letter-skips in the Torah, in a pattern thatcould not have occurred by chance.

1. How do we find words in the Torah by Equal Letter-skips?

The Holy Torah, which G-d gave to the Jewish People at Mt. Sinai, consists of Hebrew letters. These letters combine to form words.

In order to read a word in the Torah, we usually begin with a particular letter which is the beginning of the word, and move from right to left, letter by letter, until we reach the end of the word.

For example, if we begin with the first letter of the Torah, ב and move from right to left, letter by letter, until the sixth letter, ת, we have the word בראשית ("in the beginning").

However, there are other ways to form words from the letters of the Torah. We could begin with a particular letter and move from right to left, but instead of going letter by letter we could take every other letter.

For example, if we begin with the sixth letter of the Torah, and move from right to left taking every other lettter, we have the word תראה ("you shall see").

Since we found this word by taking every second letter, we say that the word תראה is found here at **equal-letter-skips of two**.

There are many possible variations of this method. We could use equal letter skips of three,ten,or any other

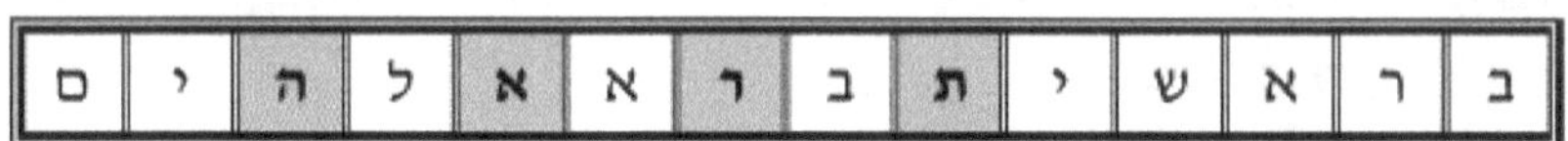

Number of letters. Or we could go from left to right instead of right to left.

2. Howare Equal-Letter-Skips shown in a Table?

Let us take the word תראה, which is found at letter-skips of two, and show it as a table.

The word תראה is found at letter-skips of two in the words בראשית ברא אל-הים. To show this fact as a table, we write out these words with two letters to each row.

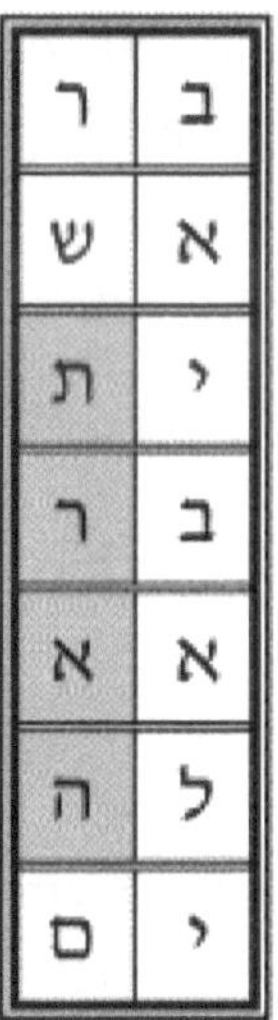

The number two is chosen because this is the number of letter-skips at which the word תראה appears. In this table, the letters of תראה appear one above the other. If we write out our same verse with only one letter per row, we get the following: In this table, the letters of תראה appear one above the other in every other row.

From these examples we see that in order to illustrate graphically the existence of an equal-letter-skip word in a certain passage, we need to write out the letters of that passage in rows of an appropriate length.

The number of letters per row will determine how the word appears in the table.

3. When we find a word at equal letter-skips, does this mean we have found a code? No. Words normally can be found at equal letter-skips in any text

Therefore, when we find such words in the Torah, they do not necessarily constitute an encoded message

.

4. When do equal-letter-skip words constitute a code? Equal-letter-skip words constitute a code only if they are found in a pattern which would not normally appear in a comparable text.

For example, it could be that the word תראה, normally appears at letter-skips of two in many Hebrew texts.

If so, it is not a code. Moreover, the words found must have significance in relation to each other and/or in relation to the passage in which they are found.

For example, the word **תראה** (you shall see) may not be significant in the Torah passage where we found it.

5. How do we know whether a given pattern of equal-letter-skip words might normally appear in a comparable text? This is the work of statisticians.

They have developed mathematical procedures to determine the probability that a given grouping of equal-letter-skip words would appear in a Hebrew text of the same length and vocabulary as the Torah.

Another detailed explanation of these procedures, see Torah Codes — **"A Glimpse into the Infinite,** "by Professor Robert Haralick, Professor Eliyahu Rips, and Rabbi Mattitiahu Glazerson.

For example, the equal-letter-skip terms) דרך הצפן‎ through the way of the code), השואה‎ the Holocaust, שואה‎ ("Holocaust"), רעות‎ ")evils"),) צרות‎ "troubles") all appear close to each other in the same short passage in the Book of Deuteronomy.

If statistical analysis of a large number of comparable texts shows that there is a very low probability of these words appearing together in such a short passage, we may conclude that their appearance together in the Torah is not by chance, but is an intentional encoded message.

By Professor Robert Haralick (N.Y. GRENDUER CENTER UNIVERSITY)

Beyond Bible Codes: "Your Wisdom andUnderstanding"

"This is your wisdom and your understanding in the eyes of the nations that when they hear all these statutes they shall say:

"Surely a wise and understanding nation is this great nation."

"For what great nation is there that has G-d so near untothem as the Lord our G-d is whenever we call upon Him? Andwhat great nation is there that has statutes and ordinances so righteous as all this law which I set before you this day."1

The plain meaning of this verse is that there are many

Commandments (the statutes) which have no logic for

Keeping them.And because they have no inherent understandable reason, the Torah says that the Israelites should not think that if they keep them the nations of the world will laugh at them.

On the contrary, the Torah tells the Israelites that it is exactly because they keep even these commandments, with no understandable reason that the nations of the world will come to understand how wise, great and righteous this nation is.

1. Deuteronomy 4:6-8.

Rabbi Sorotzkin writes2,

"This sounds odd. Is this a reason to keep G-d's laws?

So that we should appear wise and discerning in the eyes

of the other nations?

[Rather] The intent of the verse is as follows, aside from our actual fulfillment of the commandments, which is good in and of it, G-d's name will be sanctified in the world. For the nations will say,"Surely a wise and understanding nation is this great nation".Some of them will even become proselytes.

By your scrupulous mitzvah observance, G-d's Name will be sanctifiedin the eyes of the nations."

Rabbeinu Bachya writes3,

"When the nations observe that by performing the commandments which do make sense to us, the Jewish people have achieved a position of great prominence and success in the world, they reason that there must also behidden values to the statutes, even though such meanings defy our logic."

They realize that the Torah does not contain any meaningless laws; it is not something empty, devoid ofmeaning and value4. This is why the Torah quotes thenations as saying:

"This is your wisdom and your understanding in theeyes of the nations"

2. Rabbi Zalman Sorotzkin, Insights in the Torah, Mesorah Publications,

LTD., New York, 1994, p55.

3. Bachya ben Asher, Torah Commentary by Rabbi Bachya ben Asher,

Eliyahu Munk (trans.), Jerusalem, 1998, p2388.

4. Deuteronomy 32:47.

.Rabbi Glazerson & Professor Haralick

We read in the Talmud, Rabbi Shmuel Ben Nachman said in Rabbi Yochanan's name: **"How do we know that it is one's duty to calculate the cycles and planetary courses?" Because it is written:**

"This is your wisdom and your understanding in theeyes of the nations." What wisdom and understanding in the eyes of thenations? Say, that it is the science of cycles and planets."5

And to all these plain meanings, there is yet a deeper meaning. In the book ,**The Voice of the Turtle Dove-קול התור**

the students of the Vilna Gaon write in the name of their teacher, concerning the verse:

"This is your wisdom and your understanding in the eyes of the nations."

The intention cannot be relative to the hidden part ofthe Torah, for they will never understand the secret depths

of the Torah. So how can it be that the nations of the world
will recognize the wisdom of Israel?

**"There is no other possible meaning to this verse. Only in this
way, after the nations will see the wisdom of Israel in the natural
wayin great abundance and know that it is taken from thedepth of
the secrets of the Torah. By this it will be fulfilled."6**

This will occur in the near future as the prophetTzefaniah says:

"For then will I turn to the nations a pure language"

5. Shabbat 75a.

6. Hillel Mish'klov, The voice of the turtle dove, Jerusalem, 1994,
p122.

Codes that they may all call upon the name of the L-rd toserve
Him with one consent. 7

Pure language means **Hebrew. Torah codes** are only in
the Hebrew language.

Rabbi Samson Raphael Hirsch writes, concerning the Phrase in the
eyes of the nations, that:

**"... your science and art of living will form your
distinctive feature in the eyes of the world."8**

From the science of calculating the planetary courses, the

Planets, and their courses which G-d put into existence, we
maygeneralize to the science of statistics as applied to Torah, also
something that G-d put into existence.

The Torah Codes are a natural instance of the science of statistics
asapplied to Torah. We find, through the Torah codes, that theTorah is
a (statistically) most unusual book, different fromany book written by
man.

Sforno explains the verse

**"This is your wisdom and your understanding in theeyes of the
nations, that with it you will be able to answer thenon-believers
with reasoned proof.9"**

Part of this reasoned proof is through the Torah codes.

We invite the reader to take delight in the statistically
amazing Torah code tables that we present in this book.
7. Tzefaniah 3:9.
8. Samson Raphael Hirsch, The Pentateuch, (Isaac Levy trans.)
Judaica Press, LTD. Gateshead, 1989, Vol V, p47.

9. Sforno, Commenatry on the Torah, (Raphael Pelcovitz, trans.),

Mesorah Publications, LTD., New York, 1989, p748.

CHAPTER TWO

THE BOOK "KOL HATOR-"
"THE VOICE OF THE TURTLE DOVE"

The work *Kol HaTor,* (attributed to the pupil of the Gaon of Vilna), states:

"The Torah promises many blessings for the Nation of Israel and the Land of Israel, but the highest level of blessing is that found in *Parishes Ki Tavo* (deuteromy26:19):

"*To make you supreme over all the nations that He created, for praise, for repute and for splendour, and to be a nation holy to the Lord your God.*"

What does it mean for Israel to be *supreme over all the nations,* it means that the nations of the world, acknowledge the wisdom of Israel, the wisdom of the Torah, as it is written (*Deuteronomy,* 4:6):

"*You shall guard* [the laws of the Torah] *and do them, for this is your wisdom and your understanding in the eyes of the nations, who will hear all these laws and say, 'only this great nation is a wise and understanding people.'*"

Kol HaTor continues:

"When will the nations acknowledge the wisdom of Israel? When Israel are dwelling in their Land, enjoying all the blessings and good powers promised by the Torah.

For as long as Israel are in exile, tormented and persecuted, all their wisdom is characterized by the verse (*Koheles*9:16) *The wisdom of the poor man is despised.* Moreover, [in exile] their wisdom is stolen from them through jealousy and meanness."

From the verse quoted above, *for praise, for repute and for splendour* (*Numbers,* 26:19), the Gaon of Vilna (in *KolHaTor*) derives the connection between the supremacy of Israel and their wisdom:

"We learn from this that whenever the Torah uses the term, *for repute and for splendour* (ולשם ולתפארת) or the term, *praise* (תהילה)

in connection with Israel or the Land of Israel, the intent is to the wisdom of Israel in the eyes of the entire world."

Now, regarding Jerusalem it is written (*Asia*, 62:7),

"Do not fall silent until He establishes [Jerusalem] *and until He makes Jerusalem praise* (תהילה) *in the world."*

The plain meaning of this verse is, '...**until He builds up Jerusalem to be praiseworthy**.' But according to what we have just explained, it also means, '...**until there will be praise for the wisdom of Israel, which emanates primarily from Jerusalem**.'

Regarding the Ingathering of the Exiles, it is written (*Tzefania*3:20),

"At that time, I will bring you in, and when I gather you, I will make you for repute and for praise (לשם ולתהילה) *among all the nations of the world, when I return your captivity before your eyes, says the Lord."*

The term, *for repute and for praise,* refers to the wisdom of Israel, which will be revealed in the eyes of the whole world, as explained above, at the time of the Ingathering of the Exiles.

Regarding the fruitfulness of the Land of Israel, it is written (*Yeshayahu* 61:11), *"like the land sprouts forth, and like a garden sprouts forth its plantings, so shall the Lord, God sprout forth righteousness and praise* (תהילה) *in front of all the nations."*

The expression,*praise in front of all the nations,* says the Gaon of Vilna, refers to the wisdom of Israel, as explained above. This means **the revelation of the inner meaning of the Torah** ("the Kabbalah"), for the verse (*Deuteronomy* 4:6) quoted above says,

"For this is your wisdom ("חכמה")*and your understanding* (בינה"") *in the eyes of the nations,*

And, as it is known, the terms)""חכמה"*wisdom) and* "בינה" *)understanding)* refer to the **inner secrets of the Torah**. This is what makes Israel *supreme over all the nations that He created,* for this is the highest level of Jewish wisdom.

And this is likewise the meaning of the verse (*Deuteronomy,* 26:19) quoted above,

"To make you supreme over all the nations that He created, for praise, for repute and for splendour".

The praise of Israel in the eyes of the nations means the wisdom of Israel. The Gaon of Vilna finds a hint of this in the phrase (*Tzefania*3:20)

"For repute and for praise"(לשם ולתהילה), **has the same numerical value as "Seven Sciences"**(חכמות"שבע).

""לשם ולתהילה
(30+ 300 + 40 + 6+ 30 +400 + 5 + 30 + 5 = 846)
"שבע חכמות):(400 + 6 + 40 + 20 + 8 + 70 + 2 + 300 =
846)

Regarding the study of the Seven Sciences,[16] the Gaon of Vilna said:

"The revelation of the Messiah about, little by little, together with the revelation of the wisdom of the Torah, through the revelation of the secrets of the Torah and the development of the Seven Sciences in their supernal aspect, through "arousal from below" (*hitorusa deletata***)"**

[i.e., the development of the Seven Sciences in their earthly aspect arouses the revelation of the Seven Sciences in their supernal aspect].

These words of the Gaon of Vilna are based on the Holy *Zohar,* on the portion Leviticus (p. 117a), which states:

"In the year 5600 [1840 CE], the gates of wisdom will be opened above, and the wellsprings of wisdom below."

Along with the beginning of the revelation of the Messiah, **"little by little,"** all these matters are included in the life task of the Gaon of Vilna, who typified the light of Messiah, the Son of Joseph. The Gaon's disciple, Rav Hillel of Sahklov, writes:

"Who could describe or measure the tremendous concern of our Teacher for the advancement of Torah study among the masses of the Jewish People.

There were no boundaries and no limit to his concern for the sanctification of GOD's name in the eyes of the nations."

Often, he would exclaim with deep sighs, 'What has become of the wisdom of Israel?'

In a direct oral tradition, this disciple of the Gaon of Vilna went on to relate that the Gaon often said to his disciples.

"What are today Torah scholars doing for the sanctification of GOD name, like the great scholars of earlier generations did?

Many of those earlier sages sanctified the name of heaven through their knowledge of the hidden secrets of nature and the wonders of God's creation.

And there were occasions when even the righteous among the gentiles applauded the wisdom of Israel as exemplified by the sages of the Sanhedrin, Tanna'im and Amora'im."

And in more recent generations, our Teacher the *Rambam*, and *Baalei Hatosafot* and others, through their knowledge of worldly sciences, greatly sanctified the name of Heaven in the eyes of the nations."

The Gaon of Vilna continues:

"The foundation of all foundations of the entire creation, the upper worlds, the lower worlds and all that is in them, is the light of the supernal wisdom, which is "the Divine Wisdom in supernal holiness, which includes within it the supernal power from which flow all the spiritual and material powers of the entire creation, by way of the World of *Atzilut* (Emanation).

And all these powers are included in the Torah, in 'holy allusions' in accordance with the great underlying principle."

The Gaon of Vilna also says:

"The Torah of our righteous Messiah is on the level of the supernal light of wisdom, which will be revealed at the End of Days by Moshe Rabbeinu, with the coming of *the Messiah the Son* David.

Until the Complete Redemption, little by little, parts of the Torah of the Messiah, are revealed to specially gifted individuals by the *Messiah* of the Beginning, *Messiah the Son of* Joseph, whose appointed task includes all the secrets of the Torah, as is known.

Through him will come the in-gathering of the exiles, and the redemption from servitude."

The first one who achieved supernal understanding and wisdom (*Binah* and *Chachmah*) was Joseph the Righteous, of whom it is written, **understanding and wise** (*Genesis,* 41:39).

From him devolves the great task of **Messiah the Son of Joseph,** throughout the generations, and all the more so in these final days which are known as the Heels of the *Messiah.*

In the time of *the Messiah,* there will be a revolution in knowledge of the Torah, as the *Rambam* writes (*Laws of Repentance,* 9:2):

"In those days, knowledge, wisdom and truth will increase... when that king, descended from David, will arise, he will be a master of wisdom more than King Solomon, and a great prophet, almost equal to Moshe Rabbeinu, and therefore he will teach the whole nation and instruct them in the Way of GOD."

At the end of his *Mishneh Torah* (The laws of kings) *Rambam* writes that in the time of *Messiah*

"Israel will be great sages, and they will know hidden matters."

The Sages based this matter on the verse in *Asia* (51:4) which, in describing the time of the Redemption, states:

*"Torah will go forth from Me."*The Midrash interprets this to mean:

"A new Torah will go forth from Me. New discoveries in Torah will go forth from Me" (*Vayikra Rabba* 13:3). Or, in the words of *Yalkut Shimoni* (*Yeshayahu, remez* 429):

"In the time to come, the Holy One, blessed is He, will sit and teach a new Torah that will be given by *Messiah*."

From all this, we see that in the time of the Messiah, there will be a tremendous revelation of the wisdom of the Torah, so much so that it will be considered like **"a new Torah."**

The **"new Torah"** that will be unveiled by *the Messiah,* will consist of two parts:

A. The **revealed Torah,**

B. The **hidden Torah**, revelations of the secrets of the Torah.

Today, we study the revealed part of the Torah, while our understanding of the Torah's hidden secrets is minimal. In the time of the Messiah, the inner secrets of the Torah will be revealed in abundance.

That is why it will be considered like **"a new Torah."**

Any Jew who studies Torah is permitted to reveal his own new insights. By labouring in Torah-study, one discovers and shares new understandings of its meaning.

The greatness of *the Messiah* will be that he will succeed in bringing out of the Torah new aspects that were hitherto completely hidden and invisible, to the point that their revelation will be considered like **"a new Torah."**

This is the meaning of the *midrashim* quoted above.

One of the fundamental principles of Judaism is that the Torah will never change. How, then, can there be **"a new Torah?"** The answer is given by the commentary of *Ramaz* (*Portion, Ki Tetzei,* p. 276, para. 2):

"A new Torah" means **the fiftieth Gate of Understanding of the Torah** (symbolized by the letter **נNun** whose numerical value is 50), which was not revealed even to Moshe Rabbeinu, as the Talmud states (*Rosh Hashanah* 21b):

"Fifty gates of wisdom were created in the world, and all of them were given to Moshe, except one."

Later in this book we shall see, through the various tables that the Torah Codes are part of the Fiftieth Gate, the gate that, according to our Sages, was revealed only to Rabbi Akiva.

The Maharal finds an interesting allusion to the difference between Moshe Rabbeinu and Rabbi Akiva. He points out that the name **Moshe** (משה) contains three of the letters of the word נשמה, "soul."

The missing letter is the letter נ, which stands for the Fiftieth Gate of Understanding.

It is interesting to note that this difference is revealed in the *gematria* (numerical value) of the name **"Rabbi Akiva"** (רבי "עקיבא",), 395, which equals the *gematria* of the word נשמה, (*soul).*

395 = 1 + 2 + 10 + 100 + 70 + 10 + 2 + 200)):**רבי עקיבא**)

395 = 5 + 40 + 300 + 50)):**נשמה**)

Ramaz goes on to say:

"There are fifty gates of wisdom in the world, and Moshe Rabbeinu merited to master only forty-nine of them. He did not merit mastering the Fiftieth Gate."

There are limits to how much a person can comprehend, no matter how great he is, and even if he is a sage and a prophet.

But that Fiftieth Gate that was not revealed to Moshe Rabbeinu, was revealed to Rabbi Akiva and his colleagues. We need to clarify how Rabbi Akiva merited understanding something that Moshe Rabbeinu did not understand."

To answer this question, *Ramaz* points out that,

"...Moshe Rabbeinu was considered equal to the entire Jewish People. Hence, his power was equal to that of the entire Israelite Nation."

That is indeed a very tremendous amount of power, but Moshe Rabbeinu could not go beyond that. When the Children of Israel were in Egypt, they descended into forty-nine gates of impurity.

After the Holy One, Blessed is He, took the Children of Israel out of Egypt, during the forty-nine days until the Festival of Shavuot, every day they mastered one gate of understanding. Thus, until the giving of the Torah, they had achieved only forty-nine gates of understanding...."

According to this, explains *Ramaz*

"Moshe Rabbeinu did not know the Fiftieth Gate in the Torah at that time, but in the future, the Fiftieth Gate, which is a hidden secret, will be revealed, because it is a new interpretation of the entire Torah, an interpretation that no one has ever heard."

In the time of *Mashiach,* the inner light of the supernal spiritual world called *Atik,* the Ancient of Days, will be revealed.

Then knowledge will increase, and the Jewish People will be able to understand a new interpretation of the Torah, based on the Fiftieth Gate, the Gate of נ [the Hebrew Letter *Nun,* numerical value 50].

Then the Holy One, Blessed is He, will inform us, not that the Torah has changed, but that [in addition to all the interpretations hitherto known] there will be a new interpretation, and for that reason it will be called a new Torah, that is a new, Kabbalistic interpretation based on the Fiftieth Gate, the Gate of נ."

The connection between the **Fiftieth Gate** and *Atik* is

shown in the numerical value of the Hebrew phrase „Gate" ,שער נ 620 ",נ of.

This equals the numerical value of) כתר *Keter,* "Crown"), the highest of the ten *Spheres,* the *Sphere* associated with the hige sphere **Atik.**

620 = 50 + 200 + 70 + 300) :שער נ)

620 = 200 + 400 + 20) :כתר)

When the Messiah will come, the Fiftieth Gate of understanding will also be revealed.

This is reflected in the *milui,* or **"full *gematria*",** of the phrase, **שער נון**, "Gate of [17]".**נ.** It is equal to the numerical value of the phrase, **התגלות משיח**,- **"the revelation of the Messiah.**

שער נ", Spelled50 + 10 + 70 + 50 + 10 + 300) : **שין עין רש נון נון**

1202 = 50 + 6 + 50 + 300 + 200 +)

+ 5) = 8 + 10 + 300 + 40 + 5 + 400 + 6 + 30 + 3 **התגלות משיח**

1202)

Similarly, *the holy Shela*[18] writes about the verse cited above, ***Torah will go forth from Me*** (*Ishiah,* 51:4), that the Torah of GOD, will be complete and will be revealed to us in a new light, an **Or Ganuz**(Hidden Light) which had been hidden in the Torah. Below, we shall present tables showing codes referring to **Or Haganuz,**- the **Hidden Light.**

The Fiftieth Gate, which will be revealed at the End of Days, is mentioned by *Or HaChaim* in his commentary to the verse, *Water will flow from his wells...* (*Numbers,* 24:7). He writes:

"Every one of Israel received a portion in the Torah at Mount Sinai, and that is why the Torah is called *Morashah,* 'an inheritance,' as it is written (*Deuteronomy,* 33:4):

" *Moshe commanded us the Torah as an inheritance for the Congregation of Yaakov,* for all new insights into the Torah are from his wells, i.e., from Moshe's wells, because everything is already alluded to in the written Torah that Moshe received at Sinai.

Or Hachaim continues:

"Why does this verse use the term, *wells*? Because in relation to the great [rivers of] understanding that the Holy One, Blessed is He will reveal to Israel at the end of the generations, at the time of the Anointed King (Messiah), i.e., the Fiftieth Gate of Understanding — all the other forty-nine gates are mere "wells" by comparison."

But the verse goes on to say that even though at present our knowledge is mere "wells," the descendants of Israel will merit to receive "great waters," meaning the Fiftieth Gate.

Thus the verse concludes, and *his descendants, on great waters.*

It is interesting that some find a hint of this matter in the *gematria* (numerical value) of the word דליו ("his wells"), 50. דליו: (4 + 30 + 10 .50 + 6 = 50).

Likewise, it is interesting to note the comment of *VaYoel Moshe* (*Portion Miketz,* p. 331), who states that the story of Josef in *Portion Miketz,* contains hints of the future exile and redemption.

The *portion* begins, "ויהי מקץ," it happened in the End, which could be read literally, it was in the End, hinting that here begins the process of exile and redemption.

"Until the time of the end," as it is written in the Book of *Daniel* (12:9): ***"For these matters are hidden and sealed until the time of the end.*** Only then, as the next verse in *Daniel* states, ***these matters will be clarified and explained...and the enlightened will understand."***

It is interesting to note that the *gematria* of the phrase, עד עת קץ, "**until the time of the end**"plus three for the three words, equals 737.

(. עד עת קץ: (70 + 4 + 70 + 400 + 100 + 90 = 734 + 3 = 737

This is equal to the date of the year immediately after the Torah Codes were first publicized, in the **736**th year of the Sixth Millennium, **5736** (1976).

Which is also the gematria of" קודי התורה the Torah Codes"

(. קודי התורה, (100 + 6 + 4 + 10 + 5 + 400 + 6 + 200 + 5 = 736

This fits with what Rabbi Issac Luria writes in his book, *Likutai Torah,* in the first verse of *Portion Miketz* (Genesis, 41,1), where it's written,**"And it was after two years etc."**

Rabbi Isaac Luria writes that the number of days in the two years, which is 730, (365x2 = 730), with the addition of the **six** letters, equals **736** (730 + 6 = 736).

Which, as the **The Holy Ari** says (ibid.), is the year of **"the end of days in the high"**, the year תשל"ו- 5736.

The Zohar brings in the beginning of the Portion Miketz, that theword"**In the End**" מקץ , indicates to the verse in the book of Job (28: 3)" -""קץ שם לחשך" **,He put an End to Darkness".**

Rabbi Issac Luria says, the gemateria of the full letters of God's name, 111+43+106+20=671)) נון, יוד, דלת, אלף, א-ד-נ-י,plus the simple gemateria of the letters of the name of God 65) א-ד-נ-י), equals 736. The nameh 65)-א-ד-נ-י), together equals 736 (671 + 65 = 736).

It is interesting to note that the Gematria of the full letters of the ") המשיחThe Messiah") equals **888**,(10 + 80 + 360 + 20 +418 = 888), and the gematria of the wordsקץ שם לחשך ("he put an end to darkness") is also **888**, (100+90 +40 +30 8+300+20 = **888**).This teaches, that **The Messiah** will bring an **"End to the Darkness"**

It is interesting to note that the number **888**, which is made up of **hundreds, tens,** and **units,** shows, according to Kabbalah, the connection of the number **Eight**, to all the worlds of the creation.The **hundreds,** to the world of ") בריאהcreativity"), **tens,** connected with the world of יצירה (formation"), and the **units,**connected with the world of -עשיה action.

With the coming of the **Messiah**, the element of the number **eight,** which represents the **high world** above the **Seven,** the **physical** one, will be revealed in all the worlds.

In this table there is a skipping of the letters of the words, **כבוד תורה** ("Honour of Torah"), which appears near the skipping of the letters of the word "**קודים** codes").

The Honour of the Torah that was finished with the death of **Rabbi Akiva,** who found many hints in the letters of the Torah, according to the Talmud, at the end of tractate **Sota.**

The other letters skip in the table are of the words, **קבלה** ("Kabbalah") teaches us about the connection between the **Torah Code** and **Kabbalah.** The word **אמונה**– ("Faith"), in the table, indicates that the **Torah Codes** strengthens the **faith** to the **Torah from heaven.**

It's interesting that this table appears in one book, the book of Genesis, which makes the table more significant.

In this table there is a skipping of the letters of the words,עד עת קץ ("until the time of the end"), which appears from the top to the bottom of the table, adjacent to thedate 1976 (התשל"ו).

On this year, the study, and the research of the Equidistant Letter Skips (ELS) of Doron Witztum and Professor Eliyahu Rips started. **"This was the year in which the idea of the Torah Codes was made known to the world."**

This happened after **Rabbi Shmuel Yaniv,** spoke and wrote about the phenomenon of the Torah Codes, which were brought in a book, (Torat Chemed) by **Rabbi Weismandel.**Then the codes of the Torah were distributed.

It is interesting to note that the gematria of the words קודי התורה-**The Torah Codes,** is the same gematria as this important year, 736-736= 5 + 200 + 6 + 400 + 5 + 10 + 4 + 6 + 100) (תשל"ו).

As we saw before that this accords with what the Holy Ari (Rabbi Isaac Luria) says in his book "Likutei Torah" on the first verse of the Portion Mikeitz (Genesis, 41,1), where it is written ויהי מקץ שנתיים ימים("And it was after two years") ...

In the center of this table, there is the words of Rabbi Isaac Luria, קץ הימין למעלה-("The end of days above")with the smallest skip in the Torah, of the date that it was known to the world736 - התשלו,.

It is also shown, in the table, with the letters skip of the wordsאר, קוד ("Light of the code").

The Zohar, in the beginning of the Portion of Mikeitz, says that the word מקץ –"In the End" alludes to the word in the book of Job (28: 3),) קץ שם לחושך "He put an end to darkness").

An important principle about this appears in the book "Divrei Yoel" concerning the portion of the Portion Miketz:

"Matters that are hinted at in the Torah are in the category of thought, as the thought comes before the action, therefore a thought does not nullify the power of free will, so it is with the dates of redemption which will be revealed only in the future, as the verse in the book Zephaniah (3:20) states:

"When I return your captivity before your eyes, says the Lord."

The Torah hints that in the future, at the Time of the End, it will become *clear to their eyes*. (It is interesting to note that the skipping of the letters in the Torah indicates to that by the skipping of the letters, as we will see in the table of Doron Witstum,**will see clearly יראו בברור**- "It will be clearly seen that there are hidden codes in My Torah").

Another interesting passage brought in the book "Divrei Yoel", relates to a Midrash which states, concerning the doubling of the words of the verse (Exodus 15:26), **"If you hear and listen".**

The Midrash explains that the double reference to listening' as follows:

"If you heard in this world, you will (also) **hear in the world to come, from the Holy One, blessed be He."**

Rabbi Yona said, in the name of Rabbi Levi, in the name of Rabbi Abba:

"It was not necessary for the Torah to be given in this world. Why? Because all are destined to be learning from the Holy One, blessed be He, in the World to come, and thus, *for what purpose* **was it given to them in this world?"**

The Midrash answers that **when Messiah will come to teach them important information for the World to Come, everyone will** (already) **be familiar and knowledgeable concerning the portion he is engaging in."**

With reference to the question of the Midrash above: *"for what purpose* **was the Torah given to Israel in this world?"** the Divrei Yoel points out that this question is somewhat difficult to understand, since Israel must observe the commandments, (which thus requires knowledge of the Torah and mitzvot).

The Divrei Yoel answers, based on another Midrash (Kohelet Rabbah 11a), that what this Midrash means is that the statement,

"The Torah should not have been given to Israel in this world' is not intended to apply to the actions (mitzvot) **- which are**

impossible to do without the information provided by the Torah about the mitzvoth".

Rather the query of why (*for what purpose*) **the Torah was given to Israel in this world refers to the inner, mystical secrets which are within the Torah."**

These are not fitting to be given in this world in a clear and revealed way – but rather hidden and cloaked within Torah and commandments. And why were they alluded to?

In order that in the future, we will know and be familiar with where they are located".

These words are in accord with the letter skips (ELS) in the Torah.

With reference to The Torah of Messiah he further says: **"... In the Messianic Era there will be an additional depth in the way of attachment to God** *above* **thought as we discussed.**

This does not mean that the lower level will be negated, but that another higher aspect of Divine revelation will be revealed."

"The Torah of Moses my servant," is the same doctrine of the World of Creation, but not **"Creation"** as it is, but the Torah of **Atzilus-Emanation** in a garment of transition, as Rabbi Chaim Vital puts it.

But in the future, in the days of Messiah (Isaiah, 64: 3) **"No eye has seen You, O God, but youwho will act for those who wait for you".**

In the future, it is above the world of vision, above the world of thought - this is the revelation of the point of the Torah of Messiah, and there is no (cognitive) grasping, rather it is supra-rational, a self-nullification, a clinging to **GOD.**

For this reason, the Torah is called "תורת ה' תמימה משיבת נפש"(" the Torah of GOD is perfect, reviving the Soul').

In the same way that thought (the mind) is unable to grasp GOD's infinite essence, so too concerning the concept of the אין

("nothingness") which is in the light of the Torah - we have no finite, conceptual grasp of it.

"The finite cannot ultimate grasp (encompass) the Infinite."

He continues to say:

And *he (Divrei Yoel)* goes on to say: "... In the name of the Baal Shem Tov:

"It is said that the Torah is called תמימה ("complete") since it is wholesome and complete ("שלם") because only a number of individuals throughout the generations touched (reached) it, since the light of Messiah is still not yet revealed. But all of this is only *until*"**Messiah comes**

In the days of Messiah, we will reach a situation where the light within it (Torah) **brings him (one) to good."**

"This is in line with the secret of the concept ofתשובה–**("repentance") that preceded the world. Then will be revealed the concept of** אין עוד מלבדו (There is notiong only GOD).**The ,** אין**ayn and the light, which is in the Torah will then be revealed.**

The point of דבקות("clinging") and attachment to God - **which is in the end above the realm of thought -this is the revelation of Messiah".**

Rabbi Hillel of Shaklov, a student of the Gaon of Vilna, writes about the **Doctrine of Messiah** in his book, "The voice of the Turtle dove" (Kol Hathor):

"... The Torah of our righteous Messiahis at the level of the light of the High Wisdom (חכמה עילאה)**, which will be revealed at the end of the Days** (according to commentaryof Rabbi Isaac Luria as we explained on , קץ הימין למעלה**the end of the daysabove.)**

"....and the (codes) by Moses, with the coming of Messiah,the son of David, and the closer we get during the beginning of the redemption through to the complete redemption."

"The goal of Messiah the son of Joseph as the book "Kol Hator" brings in the name of the Gaon of Vilna is:

"**To encircle all the secrets of the Torah as known, and by him, the ingathering of the exiles and the redemption from the bondage of the kingdoms.**"

*It is interesting to note the words of the Rabbi of Chabad in (Likutei Sichot, Part 5, p. 200) on the words, and it follows that the **'End of days' hints at the end of the left, which hints at the destruction of evil on the left, while the end of the right hints at the time when the right will rule over the left.**

That all the sparks of holiness that were on the left will move to the right and serve it, an idea suitable for science, which serves the Torah as revealed by the skipping letters of the Torah Code, that science uses and allows for its new revelations.

The Alter Rebbe of Chabad teaches that there is the **Torah of Messiah**, which is the law of **marriage**.

As he goes on to say:

"**And understands the reason of what he said about the future specifically 'happy bridegroom with the bride' - the fact that there is engagement and marriage.**

That at this time it is considered an engagement that in the giving of the Torah, even though there was an internal revelation, we were only an external aspect, by prohibition and the rest.

As he goes on to say:

But the innerness of the Torah ... was not yet revealed ... and this is similar to an examination of an engagement, where even there is not yet an internal examination but external enlightenment ... but for the future will be the discovery of internal Torah ... then will be a marriage ..."(Torah Or, Genesis, Vayigash 34: 4).

This is the table of the appearance of the letters of the word תורה-Torah; from the first letter of the **Book of Genesis** every **fifty** letters.

In this table, in the beginning of the book of **Exodus,** the word **Torah** appears every **fifty letters.**

10000 : 13600000+80

ו י				
אלמשה	א :	א	ג
בריהו	א :	א	ג
יומאה	א :	א	ג
עדלאמר	א :	א	ג
ראלבנייש	ב :	א	ג
ראלואמרת	ב :	א	ג
אלהסאדסכ	ב :	א	ג
ייקדיבמכ	ב :	א	ג
סקרבונליה	ב :	א	ג
והמןהבהמ	ב :	א	ג
המןהבקרו	ב :	א	ג
מןהצאןתק	ב :	א	ג
ריבואתקר	ב :	א	ג
בנכסאסעל	ב :	א	ג

This is a table with the letters of the name of **God, י-ה- ו-ה-** appearing every **eight** letters from the first letter **י,**in the beginning of the book **Leviticus.**

The number **eight,**like the number **fifty, above the** 49(7x7) symbolizes the level above the physical, (number **seven**).

42   MATITYAHU GLAZERSON

ר | במדבר□□□□□□□□□□□□□□□ : 762□□□+5□

וידבריהוהאלמש
א : א   שהשניבשנההשניתלצאתמארקמצ
א : ב   ראלמשפחתסלביתאבתמסמספרשמ
א : ג   ומעלהכליצאצבאבישראלתפקדוא
א : ד   אישלמטהאישראשלביתאבתיוהוא
א : ה   אתכמלראובןאליצורבןשדיאורלשמעו
א : ז   הנחשוןבןעמינדבלישכרנתנאלבןצו
א : י   יוסףלאפריםאלישמעבןעמיהודלמנש
א : יא   אבידןבןגדעונילדןאחיעזרבןעמישד
א : יד   יספבןדעואלנפתליאחירעבןעינואל
א : טו   ותמדראשיאלפיישראלהמויקחמשהואהר

This is a table at the beginning of the book **Numbers,**

     the letters of the word Torah, from the first letter **ת** are found upside down, **הרות** from the letters of Moses, every **fifty** letters

פרק:פסוק		
	א	דברים□□□□□□□□□□□□□□□□□□ : 8490□□□+49
א : א		האלכלישראלבעברהירדןבמדברבערבו
א : א		ולבןוחצרתודיזהבאחדעשריוםמחרבו
א : ג		יבארבעיםשנהבעשתיעשרחדשבאחדלחד
א : ג		אשרצוהיהוהאתוהאלהםאחריהכתואתסי
א : ד		בןואתעוגמלךהבשןאשריושבבעשתרת
א : ה		ואבהואילמשהבאראתהתורההזאתלאמ
א : ו		רבלאמרדבלכםשבתבהרהזהפנווסעולכ
א : ז		יובערבהבהרובשפלהובנגבובחוףהים
א : ז		הרהגדלנהרפרתראהנתתילפניכמאת
א : ח		בעיהוהלאבתיכמלאברהמיצחקוליעק
א : ט		אמראלכמבעתההואלאמרלאאוכללבדיש
א : י		אתכמוהנכסהיומככוכביהשמימלרביה
א : יא		ככסאלףפעמיסויברךאתכסכאשרדברלק

TORAH

This table, at the beginning of the Book of Deuteronomy, in which the word **Torah,-תורה** appears in reverse, every **forty-nine** letters.

In contrast to the four books that are directly from God, the Book of **Deuteronomy** is from Moses, according to God, and as our sages say (Rosh Hashanah, 2: 2):

Moses obtained only **forty-nine** gates from fifty gates of wisdom, as hinted at in the verse (Psalms 8:6)

"ותחסרהו מעט מאלהים" – **"You have made him little less than Divine**."

CHAPTER THREE

THE CONNECTION OF TORAH CODE AND KABBALAH

The close connection between the codes and Kabbalah is expressed in the location of the codes in the **Torah**תורה, as well as in the number of skipping letters.

This is evident in **Rabbi Weissmandel's** findings (in the end of his book, (Torat Chemed), in which the letters of the word**Torah–** תורה is found in the codes.

The first time the letter **T– ת**appears in the books of **Genesis and Exodus,** and in the Book of **Numbers**, the word **Torah–** תורה appears from the first letter**T- ת** of the book, every **fifty** letters.

Where as, in the Book of **Deuteronomy,** the letters of the word **תורה-–Torah** appears in a skip of **forty-nine** letters.

In contrast to the four books that are directly from God, the Book of **Deuteronomy** is from Moses according to God, and as our sages say (Rosh Hashanah, 2: 2) that Moses obtained only **forty-nine** gates from the **fifty** gates of Understanding, as hinted at in the verse (Psalms 8: 6) **"You have made him little less than divine."**

At the beginning of the book of **Leviticus**, the letters of the name of **God**ו-ה-י - -ה appears in a skip of every **eight** letters,which is the number above the number **seven**, the element of nature, the number **forty-nine**, which is a **seven-fold seven.**

An important teaching according to the Kabalah lies in the order of the skipping of the letters of the word **Torah-**תורה.

In the Book of **Genesis** and in the Book of **Exodus**, in which the letters of **Torah** appear from the first letter **ת**of the **Torah,** in the skip of every **fifty** letters, from the top to the bottom, while in the Book of **Numbers** and the Book of **Deuteronomy**, the letters of the word **Torah-** תורה appear in skipping letters, backwards,הרות-

An explanation to this can be according to what Rabbi Tzadok HaCohen writes in his book "Pri Tzadik", (Bereishit), he says that the

Five Books of Moses represent the **five parts of the soul**, which are יחידה, חיה, נשמה, רוח, נפש.

According to this the book **Genesis**, a book dealing with individuals, fathers, and tribes represents the upper part of the soul,יחידה.

The Book of **Exodus**, a book in which the people of Israel become a nation of Segula, upon receiving the Torah as the source of life, represents the part of the soul called חיה.

We can expain it according to the Kabalah why the appearance of the word - תורהTorah is from top to bottom, where as, in the Book of **Numbers** and in the Book of Deuteronomy the emergence of the word **Torah**-תורה– is in the reverse order,הרות and in **Leviticus** there is a skip of the name of **God**,י-ה-ו-ה.

These two parts of the soul, יחידה, חיה,that are against the books of **Genesis** and **Exodus**, are outside the body and are used to bring down the Upper Light to the parts of the soul, רוח in the heart andנפש in the body.

In the center of the four parts of the soul is the **soul** נשמה- in the brain, against the Book of **Leviticus** were the name of **God**, י- ה appears, every **eight** letters.

The Book of **Deuteronomy** is against the lower part of the soul which man must elevate with Torah and mitzvot.

Another example of a letters skip of of **fifty** letters, relating to the **fiftieth** gate, is found in the table of Doron Witztum in his (Hebrew) book,-**Tzofen Beraishit**- צופן בראשית (page 53).

In the table, there are the wordsיראו בברור צפן חבוי בתורתי- **They will see clearly hidden codes in My Torah**. In a *letters skip* of **fifty** letters, which is the *minimal skip* in the whole Torah, forming the words - יראו בברורwill see clearly.

Adjacent to this, with a *letters skip* of **forty-nine** letters and with a *minimal skip* in the Torah, appear letters forming the words צופן חבוי -**Hidden Code**. Next to it, in the table, there is the word - בתורתיin

My Torah with a skip of **forty-one** letters, a minimal skip in the book of Genesis.

It is interesting to note that the expression **"will see clearly"** about the Torah codes is likened to the Holy Tongue which is called by the prophet Zephaniah, **"clear language"**, the holy language that in future, all the nations will realize its greatness, as the verse in Zephaniah(3, 9), confirms,

"For then I will convert the peoples to a 'pure language' that all of them call in the name of the Lord, to worship Him of one accord".

In the center of thistable,appearthe words,יראו בברור צפן חבוי בתורה
-"They will see clearly a Hidden code in the Torah".
Next to it, is the date when the Torah Codes were published,תשלו
-5736. Next to that date is the date when the Torah Codes where

distributed by the Documentary by pinlight , **5776-2016 Torah Code End to Darkness.**

In these tables, the same words as in the previous table appear, with the addition of the word ‫יש‬-**There is** - with the words, **Hidden - ‫צפן חבוי‬ .Code**

The sentence is finished with the verse ‫ויהי מקץ שנתיים‬ ‫ימים‬–"**And it was in the end of two years** ".

Two years which, as we will see later, indicates to **"The END OF DAYS ABOVE"** Next to it, the date of the publication of the Torah Code -5736 -‫תשל"ו‬appears a few times.

The appearance of **Messiah-‫משיח‬** in the table indicates to the Torah codes being connected with Messianic codes. The skip of **fifty** letters indicates to what we will see later, the connection of the Torah Codes to the **fifty gates** of Understanding.

This table is based on the findings of Doron Witztum shown in the table in his (Hebrew) book **Tzofen Beraishit** – **צופן בראשית** (page 53).

In the table, there are the words **ירְאו בברור - צפן חבוי בתורתי** - they will see clearly hidden codes in My Torah.

In an (equidistant) *letter skip* (ELS) of **fifty** letters, with a *minimal skip* in the whole Torah, letters join to form the words - **יראו בברור will see clearly**. Adjacent to this, with a *letter skip* of **forty-nine** letters and with a *minimal skip* in the Torah, letters combine to form the words - **צופן חבוי Hidden Code**.

Next to it, in the table, there is the word - **בתורתי in My Torah** with a skip of **forty-one** letters, and a minimal skip in the book of Genesis.

"For then I will convert the peoples to a 'pure language' that all of them call in the name of the Lord, to worship Him of one accord." (Zephania 3,9).

The prophet Isaiah (40, 8), referring to this time in the future, affirms: **"The honour of God will be revealed and all flesh will see that the mouth of God has spoken".**

People will see the honour of God, which refers to the secrets of the Holy Tongue, specifically gematria.

This is indicated in the previous verse, according to the Holy Zohar, which comments on the words **all the -** **כל גיא ינשא** **valley will raise.**

The word **גיא** refers to **גימטריה** (gematria), since the word **גיא** (valley), which is a low place, hints to the position of gematria which is now low and somewhat disregarded, but in the future the importance of gematria will rise and will become honoured.

It was mentioned above that the letters skip of the words - **They will see clearly** - **יראו בברור** is **fifty**. This alludes to an important Kabalistic idea in the Torah Code.

The number **fifty** in kabbalah refers to the **fifty** gates of understanding. Moses reached the **forty ninth** level during his lifetime, according to our Rabbis, and only just before he died he achieved the fiftieth level in **Mount Nebo** from God Who showed him the whole History until the end of time (Nebo -נבו) -**נ**- (50)- **נ**-בו- in it.

Itis written that the fiftieth level of understanding will be revealed in the future, and part of it is the Torah codes.

This explains why the words **will see clearly-** - **יראו בברור**, appear in a letter skip of **fifty** letters, and the words **צפן**- **hidden code-** **חבוי** appear in a letter skip of **forty-nine** letters.

Theform of the word צפן, Hebrew word for **code**, צף **covers-**, the ־ן ־ **nun**, the letter which has the gematria of **fifty**, representing the **fifty** gates of understanding.

In the future, as the prophets say, these secrets will be uncovered and revealed.

According to the Vilna Gaon, before the time of the Messiah, parts of these discoveries will be revealed, stage by stage as the Zohar (Genesis ,118, a) states:

שֶׁיִּהְיֶה קָרוֹב לִימוֹת הַמָּשִׁיחַ, אֲפִלּוּ תִּינוֹקוֹת שֶׁל הָעוֹלָם עֲתִידִים לִמְצוֹא נִסְתָּרוֹת שֶׁל חָכְמָה וְלָדַעַת בּוֹ קָצִים וְחֶשְׁבּוֹנוֹת, וּבְאוֹתוֹ זְמַן יִתְגַּלֶּה לַכֹּל. זֶהוּ שֶׁכָּתוּב (צפניה ג,ח) "כִּי אָז אֶהְפֹּךְ אֶל עַמִּים וְגוֹ'". מַה זֶה אָז? "זְמַן שֶׁתָּקוּם כְּנֶסֶת יִשְׂרָאֵל יקום מִן הֶעָפָר וְיָקִים אוֹתָהּ הַקָּדוֹשׁ בָּרוּךְ הוּא, אָז אֶהְפֹּךְ אֶל עַמִּים שָׂפָה בְרוּרָה לִקְרֹא כֻלָּם בְּשֵׁם ה' וּלְעָבְדוֹ שְׁכֶם אֶחָד.

"And it shall be at the time (just) **before the** (arrival of) **messiah, even young children of the world will find hidden things of wisdom and profound calculations at the end of days and at this time it will be revealed to them."**

In summary, this table, is based on the Kabbalistic technique of the skipping of (equidistant) letters.

Concerning the words **"they will see clearly hidden codes in My Torah"** - the letters of the words **"will see clearly"**appearin a *skip* of **fifty**-letters, which is *minimal* throughout the entire Torah.

Near the letters of these words, appears a skipping of the letters **"Hidden** (Torah) **code"** with a skip of **forty-nine** letters which are the minimal in the whole Torah.

Close to the skipping of the letters of these words appears the word **hidden code** צפן--חבוי skipping in every **forty-one** letters the" **minimal** skip in the Book of Genesis.

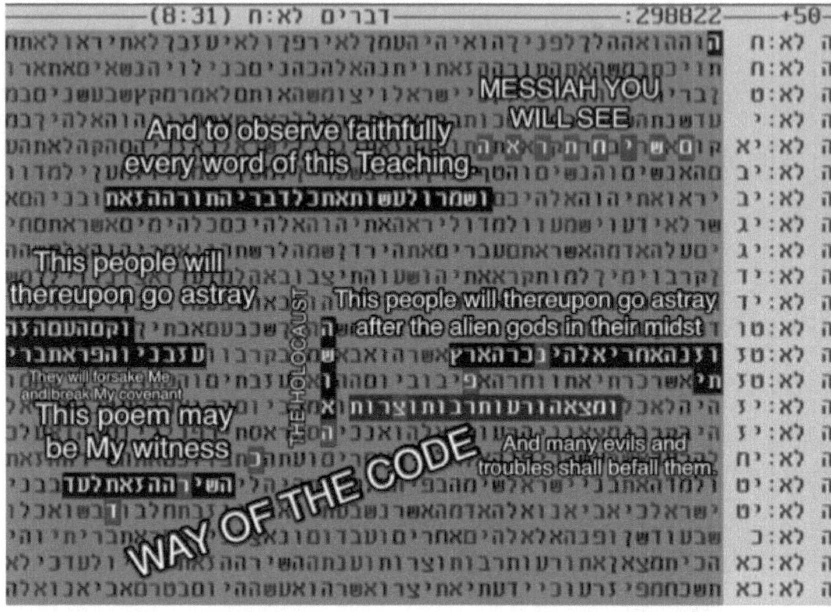

A table skips of **fifty** letters. It is interesting to note the location of the verses which describe the situation.

In this table, there is the letters skip **through the way - דרך הצפן ,of the code**which appears only once in the Torah.It appears where the Torah says that this song that refers to the Torah will be in future evidence that every day the Torah said was fulfilled.

In center of the table is the word **the Holocaust - השואה** every **fifty** letters. **Fifty** is the number of the **fifty gates** of impurity that Jews descended to the fifties of impurity.

It is interesting that the location of verses describes this situation. Next to the verse "התורה" כל את לעשות ושמרו **And they should keep the words of this** דברי-"הזאת **,TORAH**appears the sentence,**Messiah you-** תראה משיח **.will see**

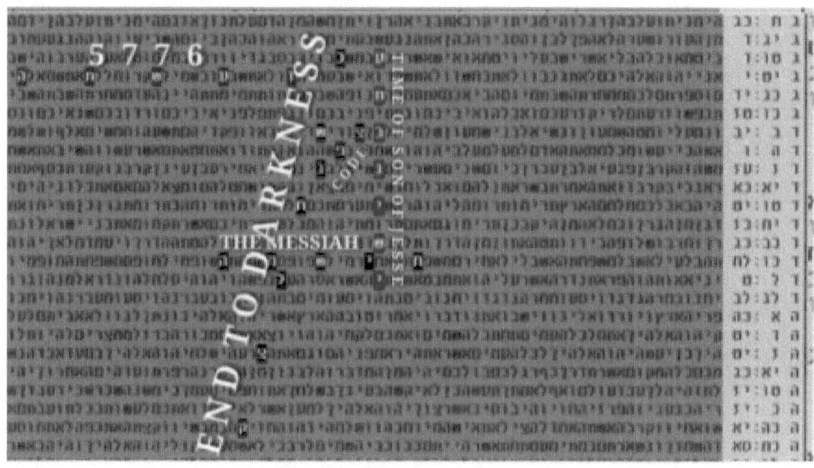

In this table, appear the words-**End of the darkness** קץ החשך- (which appears once in the Torah), in a skip of 736 letters, the year when the codes were published,.5736- תשלו The year of the Documentary,.5776 תשעו-

In the above table there is a minimal letters skip of the words הקץ "The End of Darkness" -" "לחשך.

This is associated with the period prior to the coming of the Messiah. It appears in the Midrash and the Zohar at the beginning of the Portion Miketz (Genesis) which essentially deals concerning the story of Joseph.

Another keyword which appears in this table is **from - מתשלו** 1976)-**(5(736)** - is also the minimal skip in the Torah. This is the year that the Torah Codes were first publicized by **Doron Witzum** and Professor **Eliyahu Rips.**

The words **הקוד**and **צפן**which appear in the table are the Hebrew words for Code.

The above table also reveals the words **"End to Darkness"**– **קץ לחושך**. It is also the best meeting in the Torah with a minimum skip of the word - **מתתשלו**from **(5)736 (1976). As mentioned above, 1976 is** the year when the codes were first published.

It was in this year that a documentary -**Torah Code - End to Darkness** about the Torah codes was distributed all over the world.

The other words in the table are **the code- קוד—הצפן**, in the center of the Table are the words " - **בן דוד יגאלנו**"**Son of David will redeem us".**

In the center of this table appears the sentence **End to** קץ לחשך -
Darkness next to the word -**codes**- קודים, which is next to the name
Son of Josephבן יוסף- to whom the Torah Codes are related and the
name **Rips**- ריפס, who started the research on the Torah Codes.

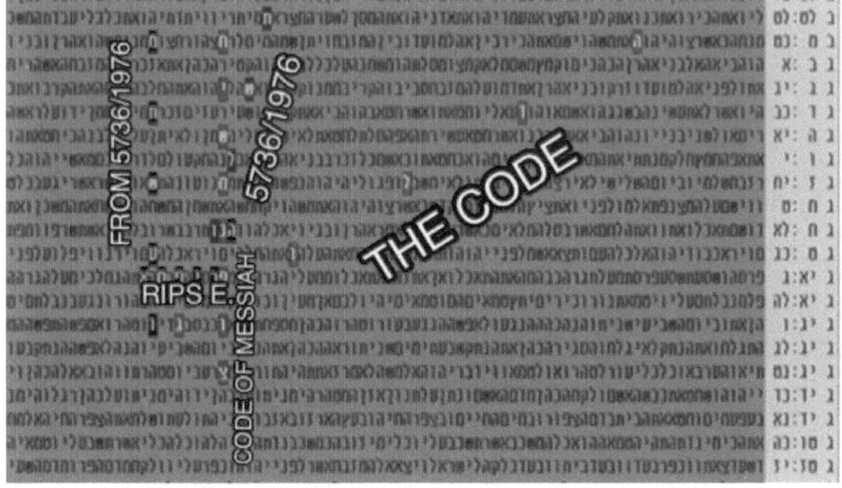

The above table regarding thewords **,Messianic Code**- צופן משיח
appears in the best meeting inthe Torah with the (Equidistant Letter

Skips - ELS) skipping of the letters **Rips E ריפס-א -(א)** (Eliyahu), minimal in the whole Torah.

Professor **Eliyahu Rips** participated in first publicising of the codes (which also appear in the table) in the year of 1976)736– **תשלו**).

It is interesting to note that in a parallel appearance, the skipping of the letters – **from 5776 –relates to the same year מתשעו** -that the codes were distributed in the world through the *Documentary End to Darkness*. The word **הדילוג--- Skipping** also appears in the table.

In this table we see the best meeting in Torah of **messianic צופן משיח code** with **E.Rips - ריפס א**all minimal in the whole Torah.

Another interesting table has in the center the words **צפן משיח** with the date when the Documentary Torah Code End to Darkness by

Pin Light distributed it as the word יופץ -Distributed in a small skip appears next to the date. On the bottom of the page Pin Light of Richard shaw appears.

In the center of this table is the sentence **the doctrine of– תורת משיח Messiah** with the word **Eliyahu Rips אליהו ריפס**– and מתתיהו –it the meaning **פשר גלה** - "**its meaning he found**".

There is an interesting sentence in the table, next to the year -תשלו **a code you should do- צופן תעשה** (1976) **5736** minimal in the whole Torah.

Also, in the table, are the dates תשעה, תשעו, when the documentary Torah Code- **End to Darkness** was distributed by Pinlight.

And the date when the research of the code started **תשלו -5736.**

This table highlights the best meeting in the Torah of the words דלוג-skipping– and the (ELS) skipping of the letters.letters– אותיות These words appear *next* to the words צפן—קוד-Code.

In a minimal skip in the Torah, the word**from 5736-** מתשלו –appears.As already noted in discussing the other tables above,this is the year in which the Torah Codes

Became publicized and known to the world.

The above table also shows the connection between the (ELS) **skipping of letters-האותיות הדלוג** related to the code in the Torah,- **The Code-קוד-הצפן**, of rofessor Eliyahu **E. Rips,**whose name also appears in this table. It is interesting to note that the date when the research on the Torah code5736 - **התשלו**- also appears.

As mentioned above, this also refers to the year in which the Torah codes were first published. In the table is also the date (**5776**) when the documentary **End to Darkness** came out in the world.

In this table the letters of the Hebrew words**Torah- קוד תורה Code**, appear with a minimal skip in the book of Exodus, and second in the entire Torah. The number of the letters in the (ELS) skip is seven hundred and thirty-six.

This is the date **(5)736 - (1976)** on which the codes were first published in the world. This skip appears vertically with the year **5736—תשלו**close to the skip:**Torah code-קוד–תורה** .

These are next to the words in the table – **'will be seen in the world'** and **'the deed of God'**. Next to it the year **5736 1976** appears.

The table also shows the word "**Ephod -אפוד**, which, as seen above, is related to codes in the Torah, providing the answer(s) to questions posed through the Hebrew letters. Appropriate letters (on the ephod) light up and spell out the answer.

Also, in this table there is an exceedingly small skip of every two letters-1976)**5776- תשעו**) indicating, again, to the year in which the Documentary **'End to Darkness'** was distributed.

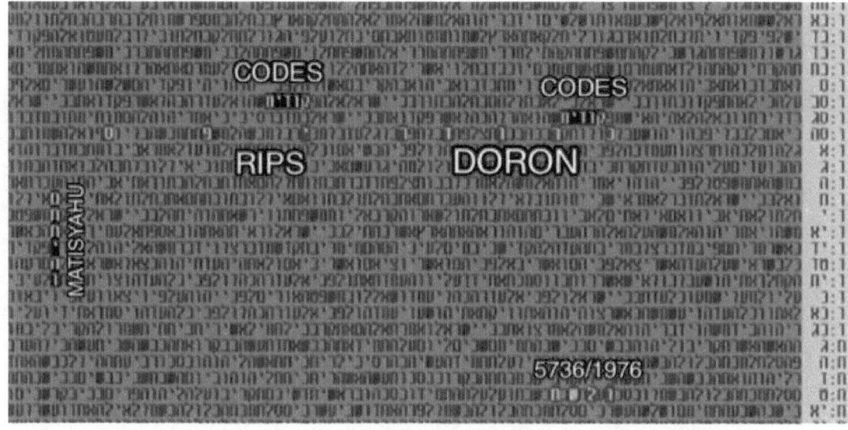

In this table, the names of the two scientists who began working on the Torah Codes – **Rips** and **Doron Witztum** appear. Also, appearing twice in the table is the word:**Codes** -קודים . The date of thefirst publication of the codes **5736**- תשלו also appears.

In a parallel way, appears, on the side of the table, the name מתתיהו who also connected with the codes.

In this table the best meeting of the words:**the'** **האותיות**-'letters and **,the skipping—הדלוג** appears. This represents the basis of the Torah Codes.

Next to these words, a small skip occurs which indicates when the codes were first published -**.5736 - תשלו**

Also next to these appear the word **.code– צופן** At the bottom of the table appears the word:**the Messiah -המשיח** , to which the codes relate.

The name of **Professor א ריפס.- Rips.E.** appears in the center of the table. The date, 2013)**5773-ג"תשע**) was when Richard Shaw started to work on the documentary, Torah Code End to Darkness.

CHAPTER FOUR

THE HIDDEN LIGHT

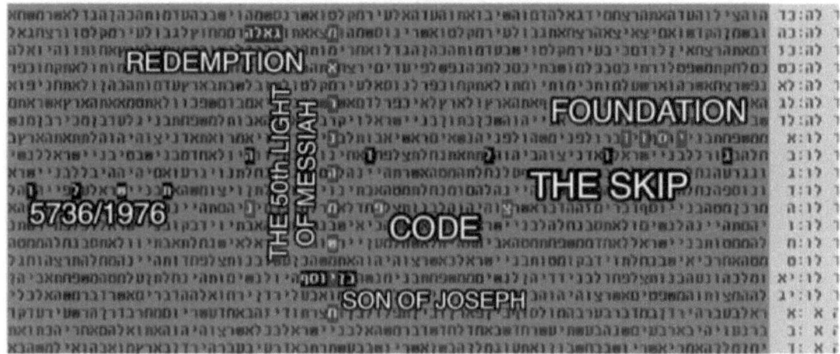

In this table, there is a single letter skip of the phrase **the-** -**אר נ המשיח**
fiftieth light the Messiah, which hints at **- N- נ**(50), **the light of the**
fiftieth gate, which will be revealed with the coming of the **Messiah**.
Next to the letter skip of the word **Messiah-משיח**, appears **-בן יוסף**
son of Joseph.

This represents **Messiah son of Joseph.**There is also a skipping of
the letters of the word **"דילוג - skip"** and the year **5736 -תשלו**, the year
in which the subject of the skipping of letters in Torah was distributed
to the world.

Other words in the table are - **foundation-יסוד** the sphere that
corresponds to Joseph; the word**code - צפן**, represents the sphere
of.**foundation – יסוד**

There is a small letter skip of the date. Another word in the table is
redemption - גאלה.

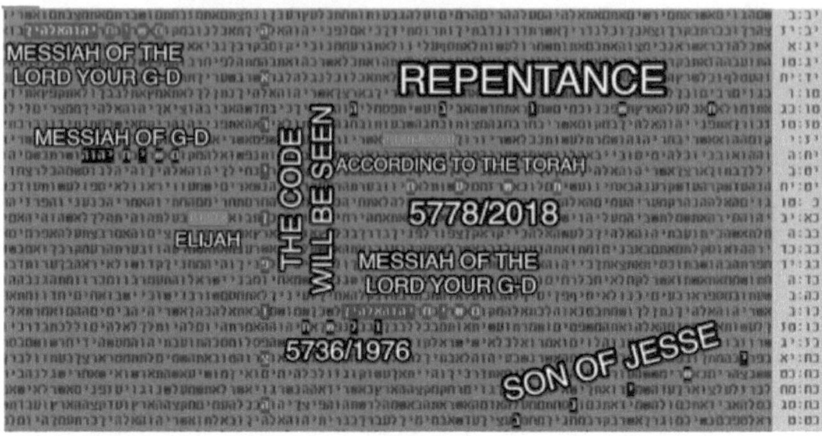

In the center of this Table are the words **The code will be -הצופן יראה** **seen,** next to the year that it was published 1976) **5736 - תשלו**) and the year.**5778- תשע"ח**

In the Table, the word **Messiah -משיח** appears three times, with the appearance of **the son of Jesse- בן ישי,** showing the connection of the **Torah codes** to the **Messiah.**

In the center appears in letters skip the word **Repentance-תשובה,** which is the main condition for the **Redemption.**

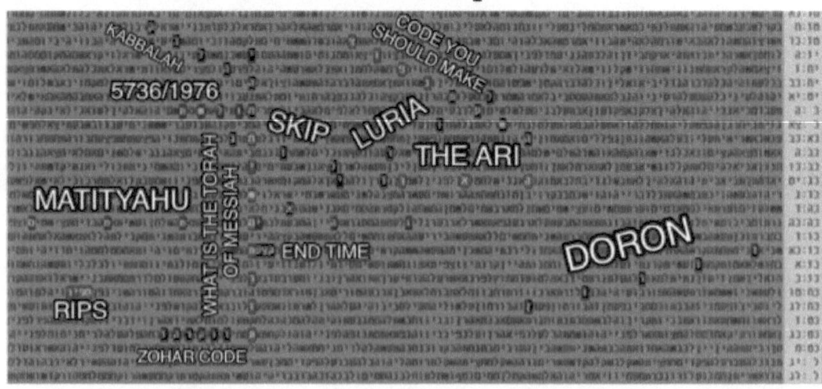

In this table, appears a long (ELS) letters skip of the sentence תורת **משיח מהי -the Doctrine of Messiah what is it ?** This appears once in the **Torah.**

What is also shown in the table are best meetings of the letter skipping (ELS) of the words זוהר-Zohar קוד-code, and the year תשלו-5736) 1976), the date when the research of skipping letters in the Torah and was distributed to the world.

Also next to the date of **5736**, appears a long sentenceצופן תעשה **'the code you will do'**-with the names of some of the key people who are working on the code-דורון-**Doron;** **Rips**—;ריפס Matityahuמתתיהו.

These names **Doron Witztum, Professor Rips**, and to **Rabbi Matityahu Glazerson** who are all working extensively with the Torah Codes.

In addition, the words **End of time-קץ העת** also appears in the Table. This implies that the codes appear at the end of the period in which these codes are revealed. This relates to the time and teachings of Messiah.

In the table below, which is based on ELS of **632**, the following words emerge: **Torah code-קוד תורה** and,**name of GOD י-ה - - שם**– כתר **crown-**and.**התשלו 5736** and-יבינו**will understand,**

It is interesting to note that the Gematria of the words –**This**"""זה כתר"
632 = 200 + 400 + 20 + 5 + 7) **is the crown" -is 632**). This is identical
to the ELS of the table.

In this table (ELS = 84), there is a single meeting in the whole Torah of
the phrase - מאר נ המשיח - **from the fiftieth light is the Messiah**.

This hints to the light of the **fiftieth gate**, which will be revealed
with the coming of the Messiah. Adjacent to the letter skip of the word

Messiah- משיח appears the wordsson of Joseph- בן יוסף, to whom the Torah codes are connected as seen above.

There is also a letter skip of the lettersskip צפן- and of the year5736 תשלו-, the year in which the subject of the letter skip in Torah (Torah Codes) was distributed to the world.

They are part of the light of **Messiah the son Joseph**. These revelations bring the voice of the Torah that they are the doctrine of Messiah which is the light of the Supreme Wisdom that will be revealed to the end of the days.

The closer we get to the start of the 'end of days', the more secrets will be revealed. **The Messiah son of Joseph**, whose purpose is to reveal all the secrets of the Torah.

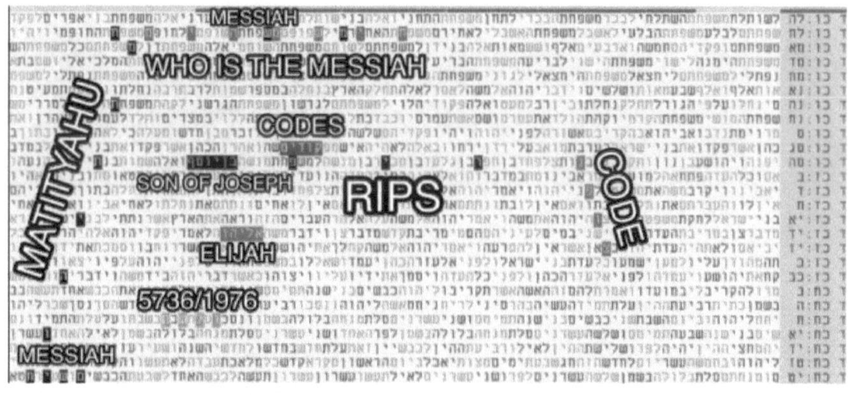

In this table there are letter skips of the wordswho is the- מי משיח-Messiahtogether with the appearance of the wordsson of בן יוסף-Joseph.

As has been seen above, this is related to the Torah codes. The name **Rips ריפס appears** in the table next to the wordsson of- בן יוסף Joseph.

The name **Eliyahu** also appears lower down. This refers to Professor
Eliyahu Rips who was one of the first to initiate significant research on
the Torah Codes.

The word **code-צופן**also appears in the Table. In addition, the year
5736 - תשלוappears. As mentioned above, this is the year in which the
research on the codes was first published worldwide.

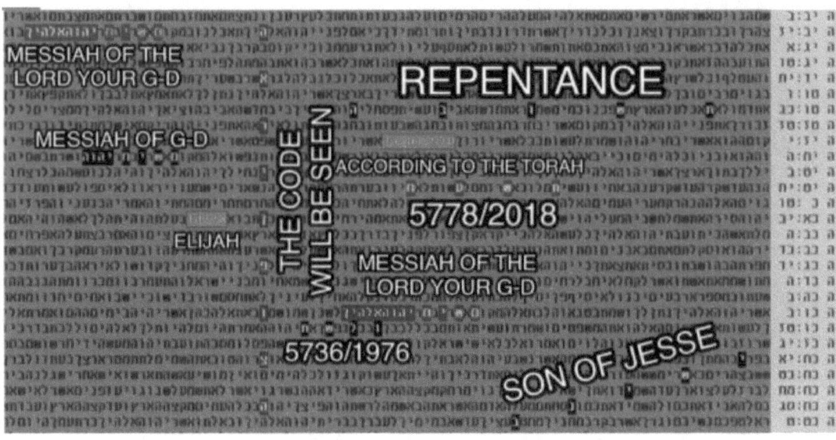

In the center of this table appears the sentence הצופן יראה-**The code
will be seen,**with the date **5736 - תשלו**the date that the phenomenon
of the Torah Code were made known by the lectures of Rabbi Shmuel
Yaniv, Professor Rips and Doron Witzum heard about them.

The words - **'משיח ה**The **Messiah of GOD** appear three times in
the table with **בן ישי**son of Jesse indicating to Messiah son of David
and the Messiah of son of Joseph,and the one who will help Israel, like
Cyrus,who was called **Messiah of GOD.**

The word **תשובה**appears in the center of the table,as the purpose
ofthe **Torah Codes** is to strengthen mans faith in God and to keep the
Torah.

In the center of the table are the words קודים עשה- ,**codes do,** next to ריפס, this looks like a command from heaven to do the Torah Codes.The skip**Rips-–ריפס** and the year he started with the research of the code –**5736** – תשלו -

In this table, the עושה דילוגים-**the doer of letter skipping** occurs once in the Torah next to the names **Rips-ריפס** and **Doron**. Both-**Professor Rips** and **Doron Witztum**- were among the first researchers who did scientific research into the Torah Codes. The word **code-צפן** - appears in the table.

The year 1976) **תשלו-5736**), also appears in the table.

As noted above, this is the year in which the work on Torah codes was first distributed and published in scientific journals.

In this table appears the best meeting in the Torah of the words-**מפענח** Decoder- **צופן** a phrase that corresponds to the so-called "crypto-decipher" - with the letters .Rips- **ריפס**

It is interesting to note that the word - **Ephods-אפוד** is present in the table, since the Torah Codes and the Ephod both provide information (or an answer) in single (alphabet) letters which then combine toform words.

The word **Repentance**‎תשובה - appears in the Table since one purpose of the codes is to bring one to repentance. The date ‎תשלו 5736- also appears. The significance of this date has been mentioned above.

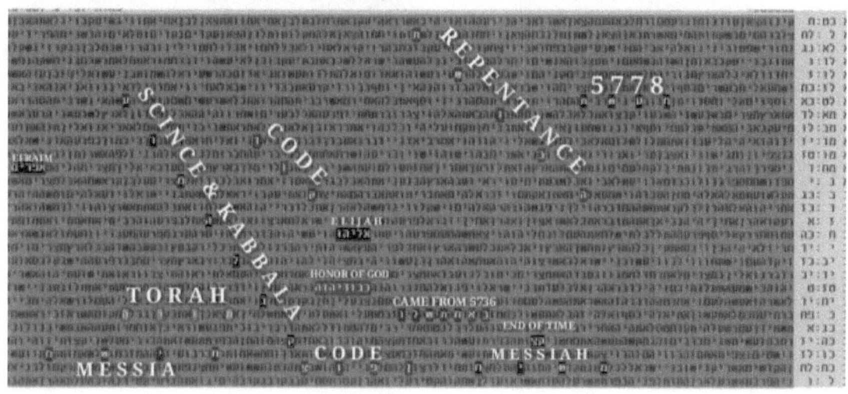

In all these tables, the words **Kabalah Science** -קבלה מדע appears in an ELS (skip) with the word **from the fire** -מהאש, suggesting that the secrets of the Torah are connected to the *fire* that existed in the giving of the Torah at Sinai.

This indicates that **Kabbalah and Science** are related to the Torah codes. There is an appearance of a best meeting' of the words-זהר **Zohar codes**- קודים appears. -from the year 5736- מתשלו.

As mentioned above this is the year when the phenomenon of the codes was revealed to the world. The following sentence appears in the middle of the table –**joy is coming Messiah** "משוש בא משיח ינשא" **will rise.**'

Also, **sons of Joseph, who are connected to the codes** -יוסף בני appear with the word **code** צופן - which teaches about the connection of Messiah the son of Joseph to the revelation of the codes. This is brought in the name of the Gaon of Vilna.

It is interesting to note that the gematria of the words קבלה ומדע **Kabbalah and science**- equals 257 (100+2+30+5+6+40+4+70=257) the gematria of the word- אור נ 257 = 50 + 207), ,(50) **Light of Nun**) Nun (50) refers to the **Fifty gates of understanding.**

This is also revealed in the ELS skips regarding Hanukkah - related to the hidden light connected to the letters.

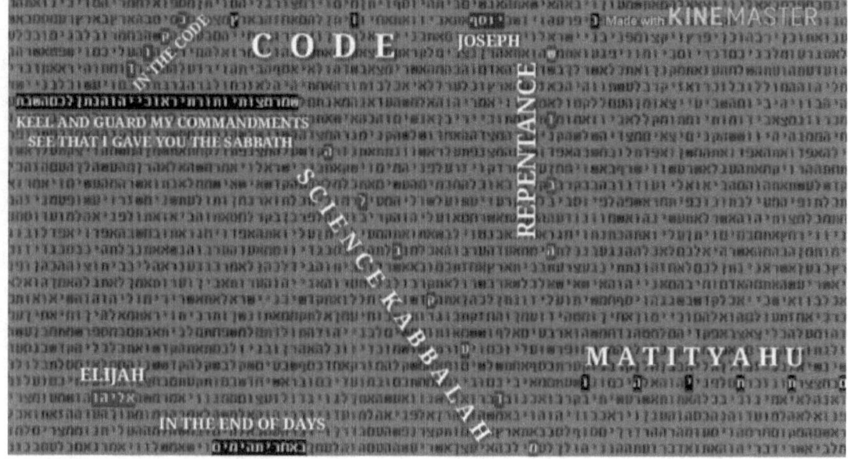

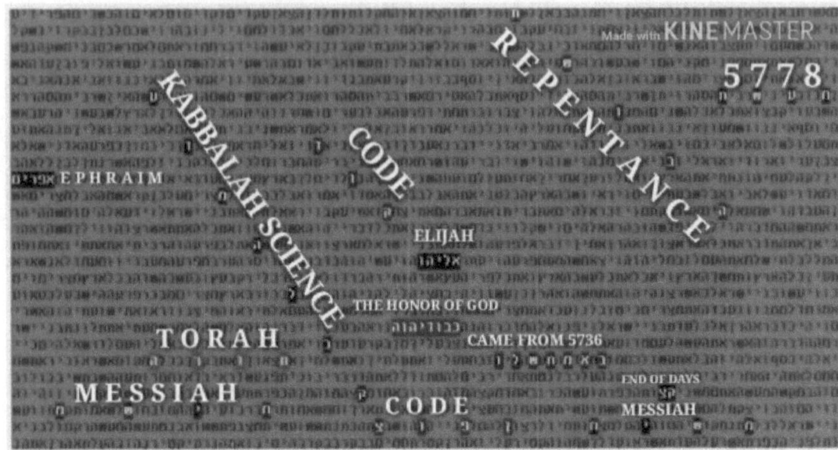

Other interesting tables of **Kabbalah and Science-** קבלה ומדע with the best meeting of the words **Messiah and Code -** משיח צופן showing the connection of **Kabalah and science.**

Other words in table that appear are, **5736-** תשלו, the date of the publication of the codes and תשובה **- Repentance,** which is the destiny of the **Torah codes.**

The date **5778is** תשע"ח a year which is destined for**Messiah** with **Repentance.**

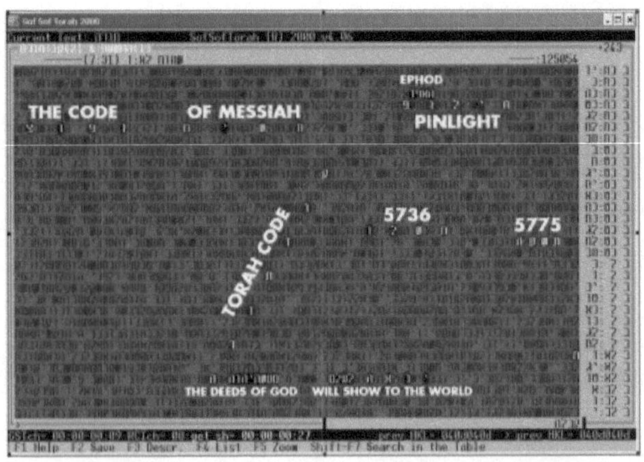

This is a very interesting table in which we have the words קוד צופן משיח **Torah code-** תורה with best meeting of the words **code** -משיח **Messiah**with the minimal appearance of **pinlight** פן לית- who brought out the documentary "**End to darkness**" on the date, 5775תשעה- which appears with the smallest skip.

Next to this date is the date when the Torah codes were first published5736 תשלו-.The word **Ephod** אפוד-appears in the table. The bottom line in the tablethe deeds of GOD, will-,מעשי ה' יראו לעולם .be seen to the world

In this table there is another good meeting of**Kabbalah-** קבלה מדע **Science**with a small skip of the year- .**from 5736** -מתשלוAs noted above this is the year in which the Torah Codes were first distributed and public

shed.

Also in this table there is the best meeting of the words -צופן משיח .**Messiah code** The names of some of the people involved in the codes, - **Eliyahu Reuven** אליהו ראובן- appear.

Doron Witztum presented this table in which the following long sentence appears: "**GOD conceal the truth of GOD-** האל צפן א.-ל-הים אמת.

Parallel to this, appears the year in which the Torah Codes were first published --**5736** תשלו.

As already mentioned above, this is the year (1976) in which scientific evidence for the Torah Codes was first published by Professor Rips. There is an ELS letter skip of **The codes** הקודים- in the table.

It is interesting to note that in the same line in which the year (5736) appears, the letters of **Messiah**משיח- and **Joseph** יוסף-also appear. **Messiah the son of Joseph** is an essential subject to which the codes relate.

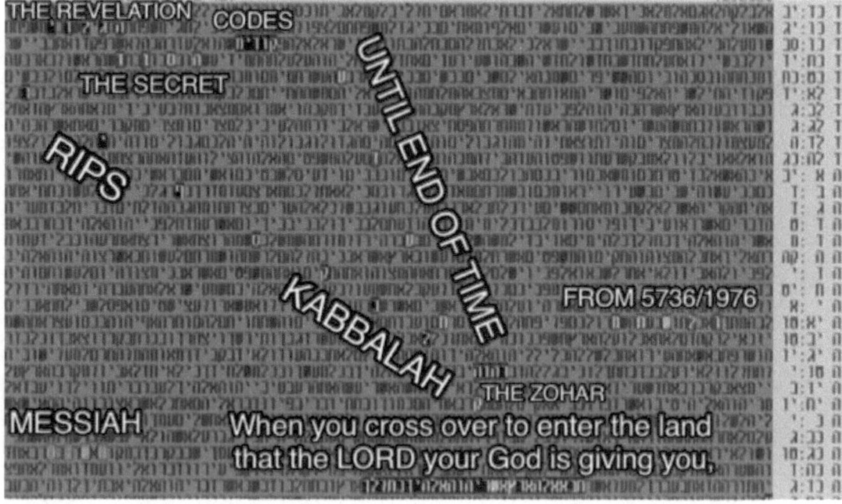

This table contains the word: **from 5736ומתשלו** ,(1976), which appears in a small ELS skip. As already mentioned above, this is the year (1976) in which scientific evidence for the Torah Codes was first published by Professor Rips.

In the center of the table the phrase:**until the end of -עד עת קץ time** appears. This refers to what is written in the bookof Daniel (12: 9) **"And Daniel said to you, 'For you have shut up and sealed up things until the end of time'".**

The commentary Metzudat David explains that **"when the end comes many will be wise enough to understand the hint."**

The Metzudath David further comments about the following verse in Daniel, **"Many will become righteous, and will convict the wicked people, and not all the wicked people will understand, but the wise will understand".**

The Metzudath David says that this refers to those who make calculations about the time of the end.

This table contains a few sets of words which are fascinating in their conceptual relationship.

The words –הדלוג אמת - the skipping (of letters) is true - appear once in the Torah. In addition the words - code-צופן ,צופן, together with the year in which the general distribution and publication of the codes started 5736- תשלו, and the scientists who started publishing the first scientific publications in that year (5736 – 1976) Rips-,דורון – Doron- ריפס–all appear in this table.

The appearance of the word-Messiah - - משיחdemonstrates the connection of the Torah Codes to the Messiah.

This table highlights the words **The Hidden Light–** אור הגנוז next to the words (with a small letter skip) תורה—Messiah משיח - - code- קוד ,Torah with the date-5736-תשלו, when the phenomenon of codes in the Torah became known worldwide.

The name **Efraim** אפרים- (Efraim is the son of Joseph) - the name of Messiah son of Joseph who is connected with the **Torah Code** also appears.

As seen above, the phenomenon of codes in the Torah is connected to the fiftieth gate that will be revealed with the Messiah. The word **code** צפן -appears also in the table

This table confirms some of the conceptual relationships seen in the previous table. The following words emerge: **the light of -אר הקודים the code** next to the small letter skip of the date **in 5736 -בתשלו** the year in which scientific information on the codes was first published.

As has been seen above, the phenomenon of the codes in the Torah is connected to the **fiftieth gate - שער נ** that will be revealed with the coming of the **Messiah- משיח** words which all appear in this table. In addition, the following date is also seen: **התשעו 5776** (1976).

This is the date that the documentary on Torah codes 'End to darkness' was first released.

This table also contains content which confirms findings from the previous tables with some additions. The words **Hidden-אור גנוז light-** appears in a minimal skip.

It is known that the light is hidden in the **Menorah-מנורה**- in the Tabernacle, which also appears in this table. Likewise, it is written in the Holy books that the light of the Menorah was from the 'hidden light'.

Also found in the table are the words: **-Zohar-זהר**-writings which explore the mystical depths of the Torahand**the Ari-האר"י**--a most important 16th Century mystical Rabbi – the father of the Lurianic Kabalah System – whose writings include Kabbalah and mysticism.

The year **5736 תשל"ו** -in which scientific information and evidence for the Torah codes was first published, appears, as well as the year–5776 – תשעו when the documentary on the **Torah codes, 'End to darkness'**, was first released.

All these words appear in Equidistant Letter Skips (ELS) in the table. It is interesting to note that the verse in the Torah which appears at the bottom of the table warns the people of Israel to keep the laws of the Torah so that the land will not vomit them out.

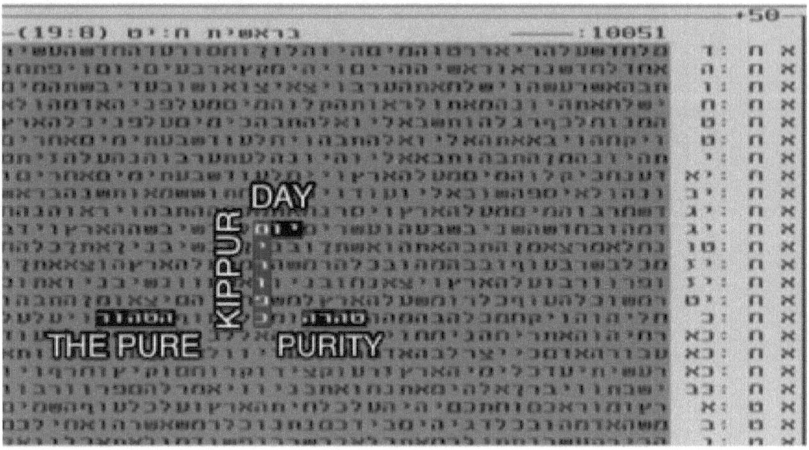

The ELS of this table is 50.

The number **fifty** mystically symbolizes the fifty gates of purity (and understanding). In this table the words **Day of-**יום כפורים Atonementappear.

This represents a minimal letter skip in the whole Torah of the word **.Atonement - כפורים** This **ELS** of **50** is appropriate for the foundation of Yom Kippur which is related to the **fifty** gates of purity.

It is also hinted at in the Talmud (Yoma 8: 9) in the sentence 'מטהר אתכם (50) ומי מטהרים אתם מי לפני - that is "before **Whom** you**purify yourself, and Who** purifies you," This is on **the Day of Atonement** - the **day** of the **fifty** gates of **purity**.

The Table above also has ELS of **50** which hint at the **fiftieth gate**. The word **Messiah** - משיח thus appears in a letters skip of **fifty**.

The words which appear next to Messiah are משיח-ישראל תשוב **Israel you will Return**-. The Rambam states that Messiah will not come to Israel unless they repent

This Table also has an ELS of **50** (fifty letters in a line).This reveals
the words **The light of the codes-** אר הקודים–in –5736 תשלו - when
the Torah codes were first published. The following related words also
appear in this Table: **.End of days**קץ ימים -; **the fifty gate** שער The
word **crown-**כתר also appears. Its connection to Torah has been
mentioned above.

אחדות האל"ה אותיות

בראשית א:1 (7:1) ————————— :289 ——— +13

מטריצה	עמודה		
ורריראאלהיימאח	ג:	X	X
האורכיסוכויכד	ד:	X	X
לאלהיימביךהאור	ד:	X	X
וכיןהחשדויקרא	ד:	X	X
אלהיימסאורירוסי	ה:	X	X
לחשדקראלילהרי	ה:	X	X
היערכויייבקרי	ה:	X	X
ומאחדויאמראלה	ה:	X	X
יסיהירקיעבחוד	ו:	X	X
החיסוריחבדיל	ו:	X	X
כירחיימסלאיסריע	ו:	X	X
שאלהיימאחהרקיע	ז:	X	X
ריבזדלכיההמיסא	ז:	X	X
שרמחחמזרקיעוב	ז:	X	X
ירהחיימסשרחמזל	ז:	X	X
רקיעוריהיכזרויק	ז:	X	X
ראאלהיימסלרקיעש	ח:	X	X
חיסוריהיעורבויה	ח:	X	X
יבקריוסשכיירוא	ח:	X	X
חורצאלהיימיקוררהם	ט:	X	X
יסמחחחחשחמייסאל	ט:	X	X
מקורסאחדותראהה	ט:	X	X
יבשחויהכזרויק	ט:	X	X
ראאלהיימסלייבשמא	י:	X	X
רצולחקרוהחחמייסק	י:	X	X
ראיחיימסוירראאלה	י:	X	X
יסכיטובויאחרא	י:	X	X
להיימסחדשאהארץע	י"א:	X	X
שאאשבחמחדריעדרע	י"א:	X	X

The Table above was presented by Doron Witztum.

The words ,**the unity of God**- **אחדות האלה-ים** appears once in the Torah with an (ELS) skip of **twenty-six** letters This is exactly the

Gematria of the name of **GOD** -26 = 5 + 6 + 5 + 10) י-ה-ו-ה,), which is the name of GOD representing *Mercy.*

The appearance of the word אלה-ים - the name of **GOD** representing-*Judgment* indicates that the basis of the world is a *combination* of the attributes of Mercy and Judgment as the verse says at the beginning of the creation (Genesis 2:4) - "on the day that אלה-ים יה-ו-ה 'GOD of *Mercy* and *Judgment* created heaven and earth.

In this table the name of **GOD** -מקום **The** *place* appears.This is a name which shows that **GOD** is everywhere (i.e. Omnipresent).

This Table has anELS of 26.

It appears in the book of the late Dr. Moshe Katz "**Compu Torah**" and is another example of a table in which the (ELS) letter skip is **twenty-six letters** – the **Divine Name**: 26=10+5+6+5)-י-ה-ו-ה).

The context (Genesis 28,13-18) relates to the story of our forefather Jacob who slept in the place of the **Temple**, where the Divine Presence dwells. Our Rabbis confirm that when there is no Temple, the Torah fills its place as the Divine Presence dwells there.

This Table has an ELS of 72

This is a table in which the number of letters in a row is **seventy-two.** The following words appear: מוריה,"Temple מקדש ,son of David בן דוד - ,"Messiah"-משיח ,"Third- שלישי ,"Moriah comfort נחמה-".

The number **seventy-two** is asignificant number representing the name of **GOD** in different ways.

CHAPTER FIVE

THE HIDDEN LIGHT

This is a table in which, in the center, appears the - **האור המשיח**The **light of the Messiah** with the **son of Joseph בן יוסף** -nextto thedate **5772 תשעב**-letter after letter, which is when the work on the documentary **End to Darkness** started. Also, showing in the table,this is the year the Torah Codes were published,**5736** , **תשלו** .

Appearing in the table in the is the word **the skip-הדלוג** which is the basis of the codes, with the word **code צופן** - next to it.

90

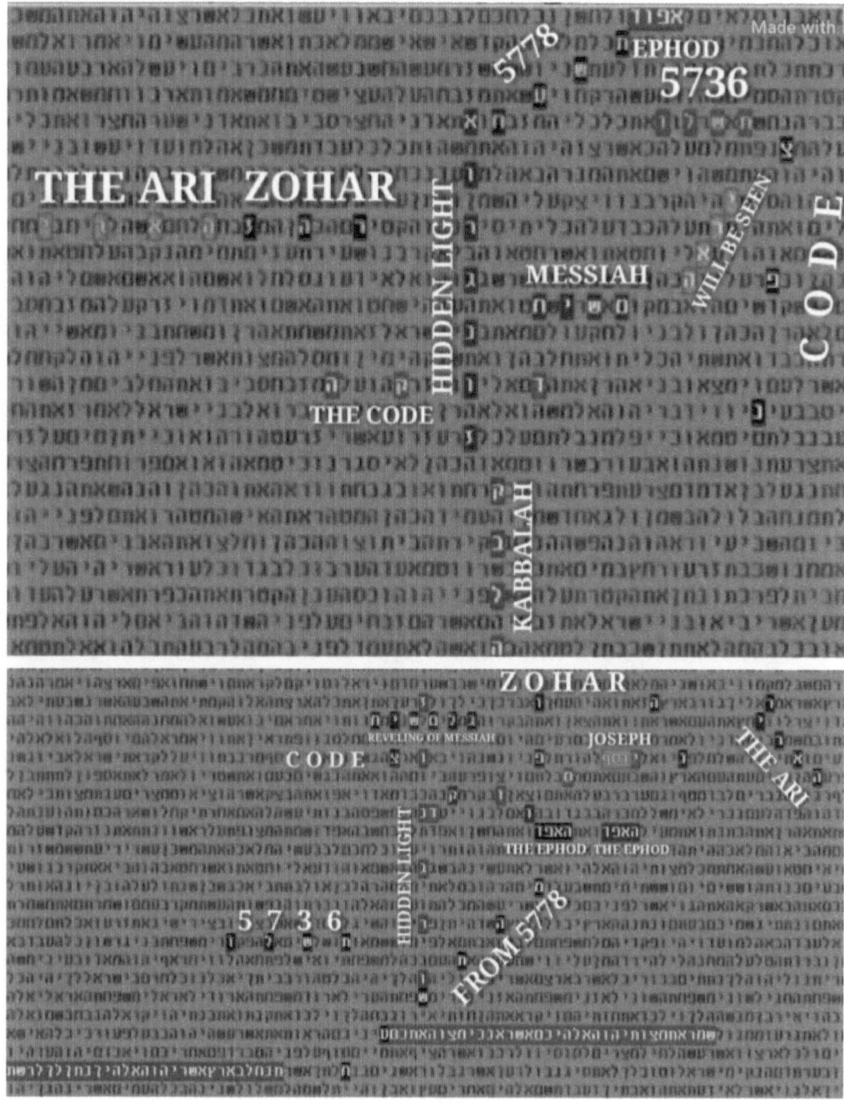

In these tables, in the center, the words" **אור גנוז**"-"**hidden light**" appear, the light that the Holy One, blessed is He, that served for **thirty-six** hours after the creation of the world and then was concealed from the world because of the wicked who will use it improperly, as

Rashi says about the verse (Genesis 1: 4) **"And GOD divided between the light and the darkness"** Rashi explains:

This is what we find in the words of Aggadah,**"see that it is not worthwhile to use this light forthe wicked, and it will be separated for the righteous in the future."**And where was it hidden, says the earliest book of Kabbalah, the -**ספר הבהיר** the book of Light, the hidden light** was concealed in the Torah.

As it is written in the books, that it will be revealed in the secretsof the Zohar and the holy Ari.

The Zohar and the **Holy Ari** are revealed in the table in the good meeting of the letters of the words, **the Zohar, the Ari ,הזהר**, next to the words **the hidden light- אר הגנוז**

In addition,a small skip of the letters**the secret- הסוד**, appear in the table next to the skip of the words **.hidden light אור גנוז**In the table is the appearance of the word**the lamp - מנורה** in the tabernacle which light is the light of the 'hidden light' as the Malbim says, Numbers (8: 2, Torah Or).

When Aharon HaCohen brought up the seven lamps of the menorah in the sanctuary in the temple, the hidden light descended from above to the seven lamps of the menorah.

This is atable suggesting that the letters skipping and the code is connected to the fiftieth gate **T-נ אר-המשיח** he **fiftieth gate of the messiah, son of Joseph- ובן יוסף**who appears in the center of the table sharing the light of the word **Messiah -משיח**, the Messiah son of Joseph, which revealed in the sentence at the center of the table is the **Messiah son of Joseph** near the skipping of the word **skipping-דלוג** and **code- צפן-** on the side next to the year , 5736 תשלו‎when the Torah codes were known to the world.

Regarding the connection of **Messiah, the son of Joseph**, we have seen in previous tables.

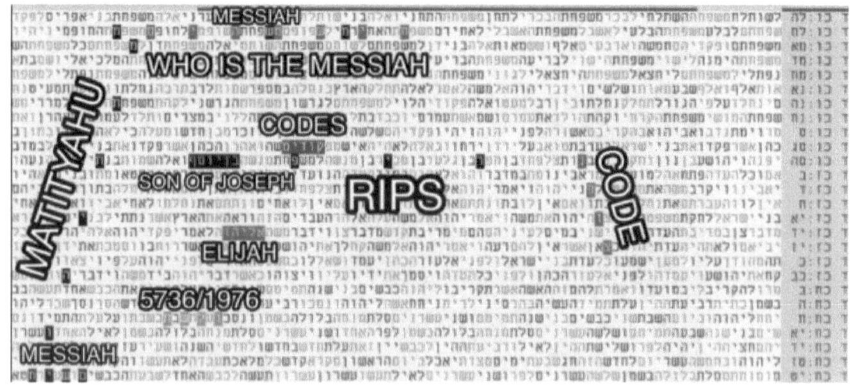

A table hinting to the connection of the **codes** to **the sons of Joseph**. In the table are the words **Codes-קודים** next to words—בני **יוסף**Joseph's Sons, as well as a minimal skipping in the Torah מי **who is the Messiah -המשיח**implies to link the **codes** with **Messiah** and the **sons of Joseph**. **Rips** and **Matityahu** appear in the table.

Also, in the table shows significant dates in the code discovery.

Very Significant Table in which the words **Torah code–צופן תורה** appears with **sons of Joseph - בני יוסף** with the word skipping- דלוג with the date that the Torah codes where published. 5736- תשלו

A table showing the connection of the Gematria and the code; in this table there is a small skip of the letters of the words **hint -רמז א-ל- of GOD** which are connected to the **Messiah- Messiah-משיח** as the **Gaon of Vilna** says, which appear next to it in the table.

It is interesting to note that the table contains, a number of times, the word, **Ephod אפוד–** which indicates to the connection between them as we saw above.

In this table we have the dates connected with the distribution of the codes,as we saw in other tables parallel the word **skipping** -**דלוג** next to the word- **קוד**code.

Table which shows the link of the codes and the letter skip to the **the wisdom of the truth-חכמת האמת**which is known to be a term in Kabbalah. Next to the words-**חכמת האמת**-**the wisdom of truth** appears (parallel) the word.**s-kipping**דלוג-

Also, appear in the table in a short skip, the scientists who started with the research on the Torah codes, Professor **Rips** -**ריפס**and **דורון**- **Doron.**

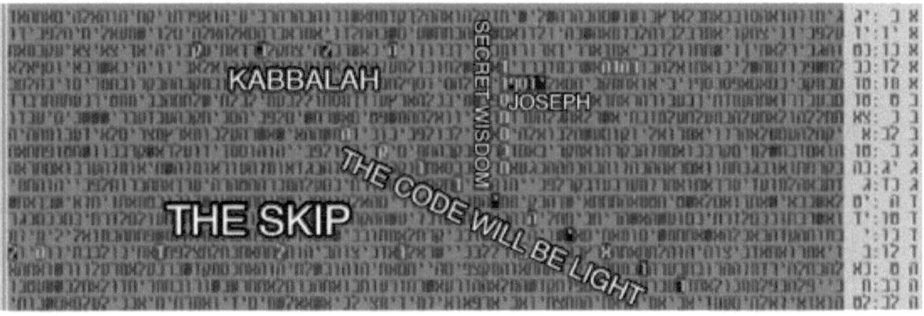

A table connecting the **wisdom of the secret** חכמת הסוד - that appears in the center of the table, with a long sentence of the skipping letters הקוד, - **the code** - יהי אור -**will be the light,** that teaches about the connection of the concealed light of the **expression -**יהי אור**-it will be light,** which appears at the beginning of the Torah in the verse: "**And God said will be light** indicating to the hidden light, (: Rashi there)

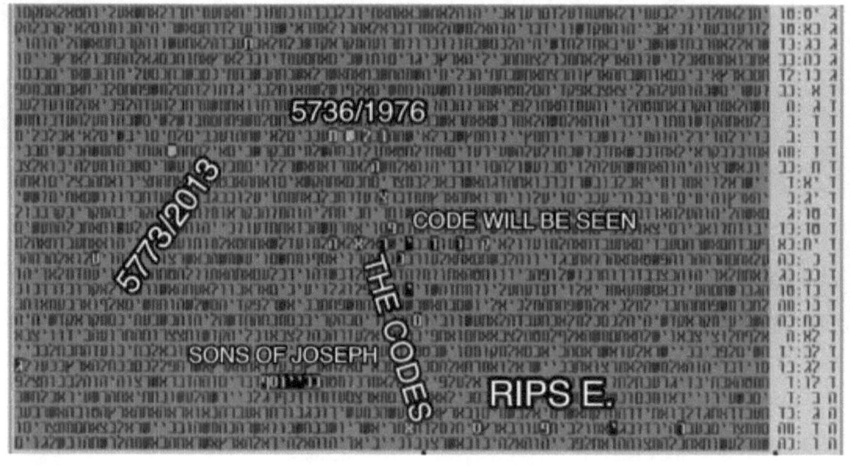

In the center of this table appearsthe word**the hidden codes** הצפנים–with the year that they were known to the world, 1976) **5736-**תשלו) the year that it was published by Rabbi Shmuel Yaniv,and the scientists heard about it, in combination with skipping **The code will -**קוד יראה **.be seen**

Also listed in the table is a skip,**E Rips-**ריפס.א, **Eliyahu Rips,** who dealt with the codes. Also appears in the table **The sons of-**בני יוסף **,Joseph** to whom the codes are related.

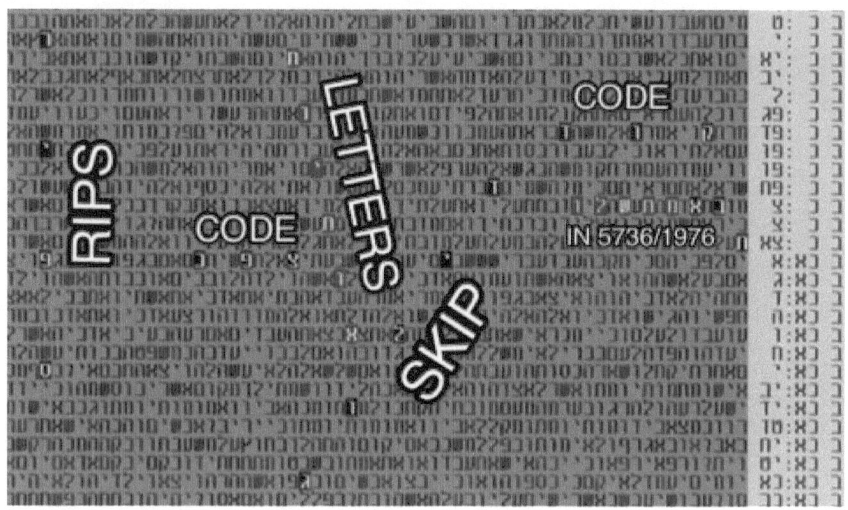

In this table there is the best meeting in the Torah of the words**דילוג**
the skipping of the letters-האותיותnext to the word **צפן**code. Parallel
to it appear the letters skip **ריפס**-**Rips**. Also shown in table is**בא תשלוב-**
code-קוד– **came on 5736.**

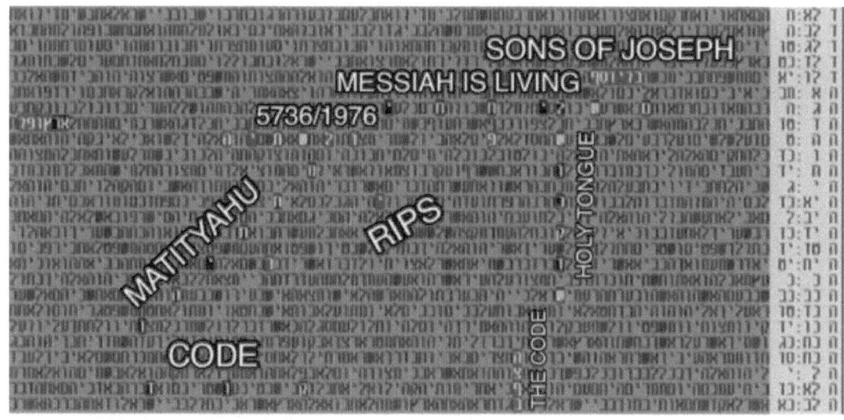

In this table we find, in the center, the skipping letters of the words,- **the holy tongue**לשון הקודש, and the word **code**- צופן this teaches about the connection between them.

Nearby, is the skipping of בן יוסף - **son of Joseph**, to whom the codes and the holy tongue are connected? In addition, the table shows the date of the year.5736 - תשל״וNext to it, appear the words **אר צופן**-**the light of the code**

CHAPTER SIX

THE DISTRIBUTION OF THE TORAH CODE

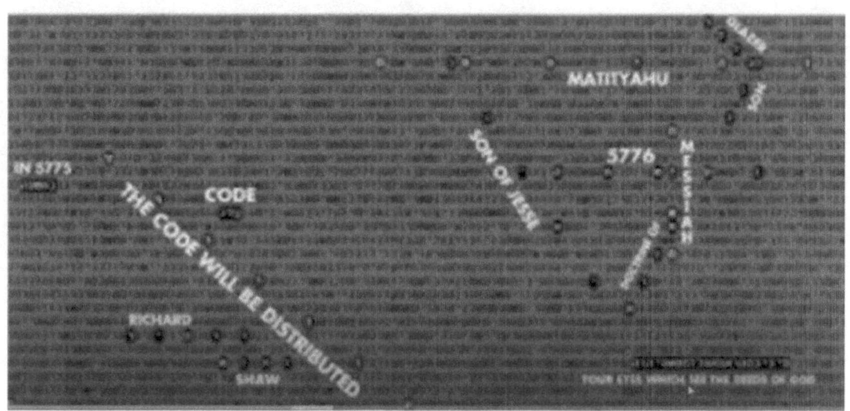

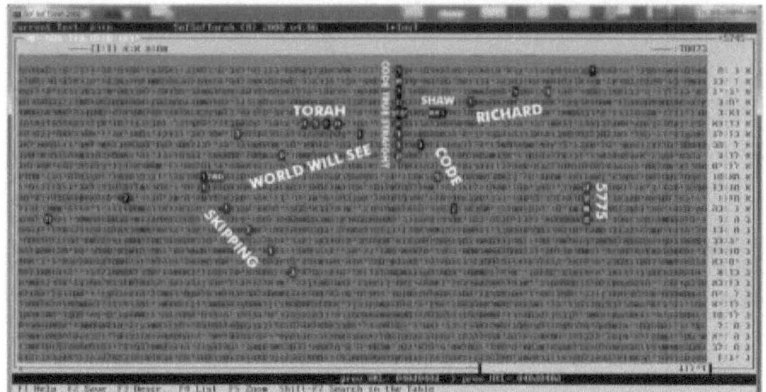

Very Interesting tables about the distribution of the code.

Once in Torah - קוד יופץ the **code will be distributed תשעה** in **5775**, minimal in the whole Torah.

Also shown in the table is the date when theTorah codes were known to the world the year, **5736**תשלו -. In the table, appear the names connected to the distribution of the code -שואו–ריצרד- **Richard Shaw** and- מתתיהו –**Matityahu** all in a very small skip.

In the center of the table,the word**Messiah**– משיח appear with the word**Doctrine** תורת - showing that the codes are **doctrine of the messiah**

Interesting Table with the names of those who do the Codes. in the center**they did Code** עשו קוד- with the letters **skip** - דלוג the names אליהו --**Reuven Haralick** - ראובן- -**Eliyahu Rips** מתתיהו, **Matityahu Glazerson.**

-

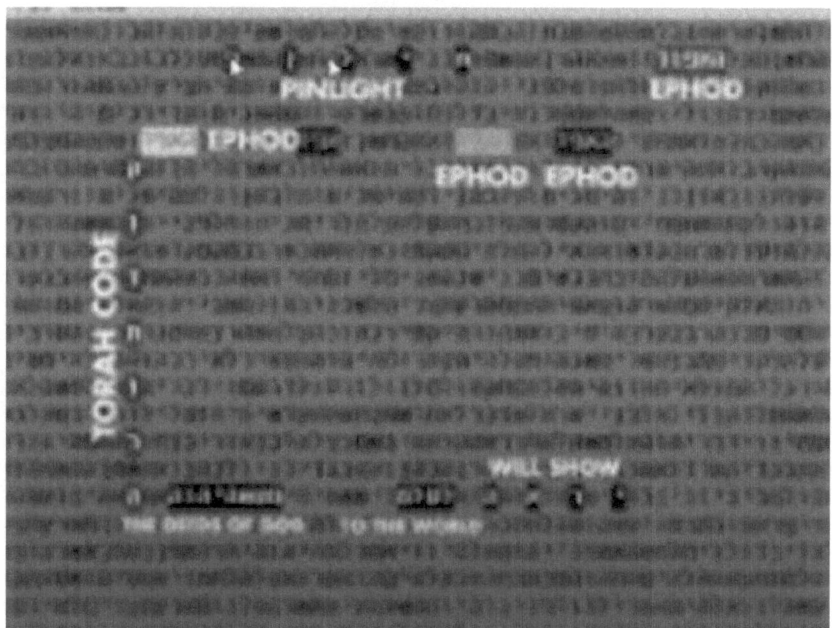

In this table we have in the center - קוד תורה Torah Code with Pin light and Ephod which like the Code shows the words in Hebrew letters

Interesting Table about the **Messiah- David the Son of Jesse,** arriving when the Jews will keep the Torah and Sabbath and will repent.All these important words appear in the Table above.

CHAPTER SEVEN

PROFESSOR ROBERT HARLICK
EDITED BY KIM STULMAN

DIVINE MATHEMATICS OF THE MESSIANIC ERA

Looking into the Jewish Teachings, we learn from the foremost Jewish Scholar, the Rambam[19] that Israel will only be redeemed by repentance.

Is there a chance for something like that to ever happen? Or will it stay a utopian dream?

The answer according to G-d in his Torah is that He promises that Israela ctually will do repent.

The word: גאולה –**Redemption** appears in the table as one key word within the text. *signifiying that Redemption is to take place based on repentance, which allows the Messiah of G-d to come and fulfill his mission.

אתספולראתמעודתנ
ועתשמעובקליושו
רדבריהוהנעשהונ
ילהאפדכלילתכל
אשרדקריזדעלפני
קרשהאחדמשלבתאר
קלפרכתויעדרעלי
הרימאתהדשואשדר
טהוראתהרבנידוב
הבמקוסהקדשיכה
למשהלאמרדבראלב
ממנועדבקראנייר
תואתהקדחתמכלוד
יסאלפושמאותלא
משכרלאישתהוכל
רבולפנימשהולפנ
שובמצרימהויאמר

This table focuses on the concept of the great merit one achieves by toiling in the Torah Codes Research.

In this table Professor Eliyahu Rips found one lengthy sentence, which is: - מי שחקר קודים זכה **He who researches the Codes merits'.**

Next to this finding, we discovered the date 1976 (Gregoriandate) which is according to the Hebrew calendar **5736** 1976 - **תשל"ו** is the year when the Torah Codes as a scientific research were first globally publized.

Other words that were found within the table are - משיח Messiah'.

Then the following words in a small skip coding were discovered: **Son of Jesse'revealing**—בן ישי a connection between the Torah Codes and the Messiah, son of Jesse..

The appearance of the following letter skip codes shows the purpose of the Torah Codes, which strengthens the faith in the actual Torah as being From Heaven. (As Rabbi Shlomo Fisher explained in his letter regarding Torah Codes) With the word: -**Code**- -צפן and the word:'**Faith**-אמונה as we see in the Table below.

These two tables could demonstrate that the Torah codes allow one to strengthen their faith in G-d to a point which one therefore merits the coming of Messiah, Son of David.

Rabbi Isaac Luria

To understand Torah codes, one must certainly know where they come from, according to classic Jewish teachings and according to the Sages, Torah codes area part of Kabbalah. The Zohar the chief text of Kabbalah contains the hidden aspects and teachings of the Torah.

And the ultimate Chief expounder of this knowledge was a man called Isaac (Ben Solomon) **Luria Ashkenazi** (1534–July 25, 1572) (Hebrew[1]: יִצְחָקבן שלמה לוּרְיָא אשכנזי *Yitzhak Ben Sh'lomoLurya Ashkenazi*), commonly known in Jewish religious circles as "**Ha'ARI**" (meaning "The Lion"), "**Ha'ARI Hakadosh**" [the holy ARI] "**ARI ZaL**" [the ARI, Of Blessed Memory]

The Ari was a foremost Rabbi and Jewish msytic in the community of city Safad in the Galilee[2] region of ottoman Syria[3]. He is in his capacity considered the father of contemporary Kabbalah[4] and his teachings are being referred to as Lurianic Kabbalah[5].

While his direct literary contribution to the Kabbalistic school of Safed was extremely minute (he wrote only a few poems), his spiritual fame led to their veneration and the acceptance of his authority. The works of his disciples compiled his oral teachings into writing.

Every custom of the Ari was scrutinized, and many were accepted, even against previous practice.Luria died at Safed on July 25, 1572, and is buried at the Old Jewish Cemetery, Safed.

The Ari Ashkenazi Synagogue[6], located in Safed, Israel, was built in memory of Luria during the late 16th century.

---

1.   https://en.wikipedia.org/wiki/Hebrew_language

2.   https://en.wikipedia.org/wiki/Galilee

3.   https://en.wikipedia.org/wiki/Ottoman_Syria

4.   https://en.wikipedia.org/wiki/Kabbalah

5.   https://en.wikipedia.org/wiki/Lurianic_Kabbalah

6.   https://en.wikipedia.org/wiki/Ari_Ashkenazi_Synagogue

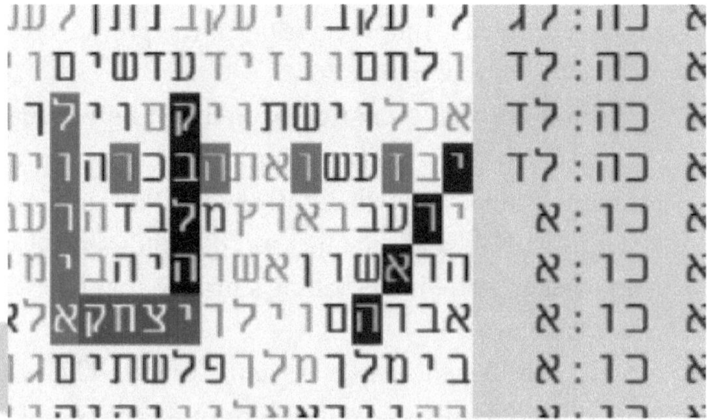

This significant small table was found about Rabbi Luria. It has in parallel rows ELS of the words: **'Luria לוריא**and the words: **קוד-'Code'**.and the word: **יצחק** of Isaac, pronounced **'Yitzchak'**And the word: **'The Ari- הארי**The foremost known acronym for the name of Rabbi Yitzchak Luria.

Rabbi Moshe Cordovero

Torah Code Table by Doron Witzum

Moses ben Jacob Cordovero (משהקורדובירו *Moshe Kordovero* ; 1522–1570) was a central figure in the historical development of Kabbalah[7].

He was a leader of a mystical school in 16th-century Safed, Ottoman Syria. He is known by the acronym the **Ramak** (רמ״ק).

After the medieval flourishing of Kabbalah[8], centered on the Zohar, attempts were made to give a complete intellectual system to its theology, such as by Meir ibn Gabbai[9].

Influenced by the earlier success of Jewish philosophy[10] in articulating a rational study of Jewish thought, Moshe Cordovero

---

7.	https://en.wikipedia.org/wiki/Kabbalah

8.	https://en.wikipedia.org/wiki/Kabbalah

9.	https://en.wikipedia.org/wiki/Meir_ben_Ezekiel_ibn_Gabbai

10.	https://en.wikipedia.org/wiki/Jewish_philosophy

produced the first full integration of the previous differing schools in Kabbalistic interpretation.

While he was a mystic inspired by the opaque imagery of the Zohar, *Cordoverian Kabbalah* utilised the conceptual framework of evolving[11] cause and effect[12] from the Infinite[13] to the Finite[14] in systemising Kabbalah, the method of philosophical style discourse he held most effective in describing a process that reflects sequential logic and coherence.

His encyclopedic works became a central stage in the development of Kabbalah.Immediately after him in Safed; Isaac Luria[15] articulated a subsequent system of Kabbalistic theology, with new supra-rational doctrines recasting previous Kabbalistic thought.

While Lurianism displaced the Cordoverian scheme and became predominant in Judaism, its followers read Cordoverian works in harmony with their teachings.

Where to them, Lurianism described the World" of Rectification[16], Cordovero described the pre-Rectification of the "World".Botharticulations of the 16th century mystical Renaissance were given birth to in Safed.

A hidden Torah Code table about this foremost scholar and kabbalist was found within the Torah.

11.   https://en.wikipedia.org/wiki/Emanationism

12.   https://en.wikipedia.org/wiki/Ohr

13.   https://en.wikipedia.org/wiki/Ein_Sof

14.   https://en.wikipedia.org/wiki/Four_Worlds

15.   https://en.wikipedia.org/wiki/Isaac_Luria

16.   https://en.wikipedia.org/wiki/Tikun_(Kabbalah)

אמלבדההרעבהראשון
ספוגסעליהויקראשמי
שאנמצוהאתרלנאל
דיצמלכאיוקסאביריו
זגרירשאנתואלהיםלא
ימהבארהואישקוהעד
חלעבדתיעמךלמהרמי
ודאיבנרותאמרלההמעט
כינוובינייעקבויעקבר
והארץהזאתושבאלארץ
אליחרבעיניאדניכילו
וישכסלבןבבקרוינשקל
ושרבמצאכמאתואמרתם
יחובעיניךרולקחתמנחת
נערלאשהויענובנייעק

In the center of this table the best meeting of the ELSs of the words: **Rabbi Moshe'and** רבי משה- the word: קורדוברו-**Cordovero'and** the word: הרמק, **HaRamak'**, the acronym for **Rabbi Moshe Cordovero.** These are the words that were found.

Interesting to note is that the acronym for his name HaRamak'appears parallel to his name.It is the Ramak himself who refers in his book *Pardes Rimonim* to the numerous ways the hidden meanings of the allusions of Torah can be deciphered.And just paralellel to the word **Cordovero'**appears the word: צופן **-Code.**

And there were more hidden codes about Rabbi Luria, the Zohar and Kabbalah found within the Torah text. We find at the top of table in a very good meeting of words, the key words: זוהר-יצחק- לוריא- **'Luria, Kabbalah, Zohar, Yitzchak** -קבלה-.

The word: **'Code'**-קוד and the word: **'Skip**-דילוג also appears in the same table.

Demonstrating that the great Masters of Kabbalah, who taught about the hidden meanings of the Torah, coud be connected if not entrusted with the Torah codes as a messianic, redemptive system. As is known in Judaism, only very few were and can know the most hidden things.

Reflection of Reality

For marvellous events in history to be recognized it depends on the degree to which everyone contemplates them.

Therefore, the Jewish teachings say: One who does not give any thought to the coming of the Messiah will not notice anything at all.'

It further says, Sometimes events of sublime importance occur, but people do not recognize their significance.'

This phenomenon in itself is also mentioned by a foremost disciple of the Jewish Scholar,'The Gaon of Vilna',Rabbi Hillel of Sh'klov, in the book called קול התור -The **Voice of The Turtle Dove**,'New edition, p. 50), he states: " **Joseph recognized his brothers, but they did not recognize him**)Genesis 42:8(

This is one of the functions of **Joseph**, not only in his own generation when he lived, but in every generation the Messiah Son of Joseph, - משיח בן יוסף

Recognizes his fellow Jews, but they do not recognize him.

This is a stratagem of an Obstructer (The Satan[20] , who'his'job is it to hide the characterstics of the first Messiah[21] known as Messiah Son of Joseph, so that people do not recognize the events of the era of this Josephic process'that are known as the **Heels of the Messiah**' and even regard these events as insignificant due to our many sins.

Where it not for this, our suffering would have already ended. If the Nation of Israel would recognize Joseph at the time known as the

'Heels of the Messiah'allowing for the descend of Joseph -namely the ingathering of the Exiles – we would have been already redeemped with a complete redemption.'

This type of blindness/ concealment also ranslates to other aspects of Kabbalah that are vital to the understanding of Torah Codes, such as the gematria. (/gəˈmeItriə/[17]; **גמטריא**, plural גימטריאות, *gematriot)*is an alphanumeric code of assigning a numerical value to a name, word or phrase based on its Hebrew letters.

A single word can yield multiple values depending on the cipher[18] used.

The Baal Ha Roke'ach[22] (As well as in the Me'AmLo'ez[23] commentary) gives a similar explanation to why some individuals deem it necessary to belittle the significance of Gematria,(To learn more about this form of interpretation of the Torah refer to our book *Through The Lense of Gematria'*),

The Baal HaRockeach cites the verse in Deuteronomy (32:47) **"The Torah] is not an empty matter for you. כי לא -דבר רק הוא מכם** .In this verse we find a direct reference to this issue:

If we add up the numerical values of the entire letters in this phrase, the total is **679'**, which equals the numerical value of the word: **'Gematriot'גימטריאות**(Plural Hebrew term of Gematria). **כי לא -דבר** 679 679=30+31+206+300+12+100**רק הוא מכם** 679=1+ 3+10+40+9+200+10+6+400)-**גמטריאות)**

Allowing us to see that the Torah hints to us that Gematria are not an empty matter before us.

Vital to know is also that the word **מכם**means literally **'From you'**. The Sages expound this verse to hint to us: **If this is empty, its emptiness is <u>from you.</u>**'(Jerusalem Talmud Torah, Pe'ah 3:1)

---

17.   https://en.wikipedia.org/wiki/Help:IPA/English

18.   https://en.wikipedia.org/wiki/Cipher

In other words, if one feels that Gematria (Gematriot – Numerical Values) is an empty matter of no significance, one should know that the source of this feeling is **"from oneself"**, because oneself is empty.

The Prophet Joel speaks about the possibility of seeing and explaining one and the same matter in two opposite ways:

'The paths of G-d are straight. The righteous walk in them and the sinful stumble in them.' (Joel 14:10).

Similarly, the Sages note on the following verse, **This is the Torah which Moses placed before the Children of Israel.**(Deuteronomy 4:44)

That the word in Hebrew for placed is שם (sam(, which is almost identical to the Hebrew word –) סםsam).

What is the significance? סם (sam) means English:'**Drug, medicine, elixir.**'Hence, the Sages expound this verse to hin to us:

'"If one merits, it [The Torah] becomes and elixir of life for him; but if he does not merit, it becomes an elixir of death for him"'.(Yuma 72:b).

The commentators explain that the Sages' term, **If one merits'**means,**If one is sufficiently pure'**.

That is, if ones character traits are pure and good, he will understand the words of the Torah in the right way and they will be an elixir of life for him, but if his character traits are not pure he will interpret the Torah'teachings in a twisted manner and they will be an **elixir** (סם) of death for him.

The fact that there are those who belittle the importance of Gematria is according to the Sages one of the prophetic signs of the time period in history called in Hebrew '**Ikveta DeMeshicha**' - עקבתא דמשיחא, **The Heels of the Messiah**'. The Sages inform us (Sotah 49:b; Sanhendrin 97b) that during that time period,

" The wisdom of the scribes will become repugnant. חכמת הסופרים תסרח. On the other hand, it is interesting to note how the foremost Jewish Scholar the Ben Ish Chai[24]explains this statement in his work,**Ben Yehoyada'**)In regards to the Tractate Sanhedrin).

The Ben Ish Chai interprets the word **תסרח** as not meaning **Repugnant'**, but insteadas**'Expanding, increasing'**As in Exodus 26:12, where the exact verb is used to describe the extra length of the curtain is extending beyond the rest.

Based on this interpretation, one of the signs of the approaching of the Messiah is the <u>expansion</u> of **the wisdom of the scribes.**

> The actual word for **Scribes'סופרים** (Sofrim), also carries the meaning of Those who count', i.e., for those who count the letters of the Torah. Weather in the form of Gematria or Equal – **Letter – Skip Codes**– two forms of wisdom that are ever expanding in fullness in our day.

> To these seemingly contradictory interpretations of the Sages' dictum, **"The wisdom of the scribes will become repugnant"**- ""**חכמת הסופרים תסרח**"

> Or alternatively, **the wisdom of the scribes will expand and increase.** One may apply the expression: **Both these and those are the words of the living G-d.'**

> Both the positive and the negative interpretation are being fulfilled in our generation in relation to the Torah Codes.

Torah Codes -Letter Skip

This is a vital teaching for the actual 'Skip Code findings' in the Torah.

In this Torah Code table we find the best meeting of words in the entireTorah, for the word, - הדילוגים **The skips**'and the words , קודים הם **They are codes**'.

So, what should this all mean to us one may ask?

The notion that a Divine athematics'undergirds nature is the basis of all ideas that goes back to kabbalistic sources as well as the Platonic sources.

To expound on the Jewish thought regarding this concept, Judaism teaches that all reality is composed of a **DNA** made up of the 22 letters of the Hebrew Alphabet, that constitutes it as the **Holy Tongue'-לשון הקודש-Lashon Ha Kadosh.**'It is a divine language that is not just spoken to communicate, but is alsoalanguage/ letters -DNA program that constitutes the mere fabric of reality itself.

And it is with G-ds 10(ten) utterances, that are constantly spoken by Him that He sustains all Creation.

The Torah itself is also according to this Tradition the **Blueprint of Creation.**'That means that G-d investigatethe Torah to create the world, like an architect would look into his architectual blueprint plans before he builds a house from its foundation to the top.

And it was proclaimed by the 18th Century Jewish Scholar and Sage called The **Vilna Gaon** to underline this concept that:

"The rule is that all that was, is, and will be unto the End of Time is included in the Torah, from the first word to the last word."

And not merely in a general sense, but as to the details of every species and each one individually, and details of details of everything that happened to him from the day of his birth until his end.'

Torah Codes as such hold the key and allow us to look through this divine mathematical and kabbalistic telescope into the thought that goes into Creation by the Creator Himself.

Chapter 8

THE PURPOCE OF THE TORAH CODE

Code purpose allows us to explore the world of Torah Codes to understand their purpose, their structure, and their content.

There are some skeptics, who for various reasons, hold the hypothesis that Torah codes are not real and all that has been noticed is in fact just something that has happened by chance arrangements of letters.

We hold a different hypothesis. We hold the hypothesis that the letterarrangements constituting Torah codes are unexpected and do not occur by chance.

The exploration that we do in the world of Torah Codes here is not for the purpose of making formal experiments to evaluate the probability that something might happen by chance.

Nor is it to formally test the Null hypothesis of "No Torah code effect"against some alternative hypothesis. Such formal experiments and testing are important and must be done.

It is a place where we can write our thoughts and review what we have done in some organized format. We do this in order to help us think of formal hypotheses to test that which will get us to the next level of understanding this phenomenon.

And we do this in a way that can be shared with others.In our disciplined exploration, we do in fact use formal tools and do evaluate with Monte Carlo experiments the probability that as good as a table as we have found might occur by chance.

These experiments are done within the entire Torah text, also known as the Five Books of Moses. We use the Koren edition.

All our Monte Carlo experiments are done in the ELS random placement text population and the measure of the compactness of a table that we use is the table area, the number of rows of the table times the number of columns of the table.

We know that the table area measure is certainly not the most sensitive.

In fact, our formal experiments seem to indicate that it is among the least sensitive. But we use it here because it is the easiest for us and others to understand.

When we use it, we do not need to express what we are doing in technical mathematics.

On the one hand our use of the area as compactness may be a major shortcoming because of its lack of sensitiveness.

On the other hand, it may be a major advantage because it will keep us playing, for now, where the phenomena appear at its strongest.

So, we have less of an issue distinguishing signal from noise.

Our experimental protocol nearly always has the maximum row skip and maximum column skip for an ELS on a cylinder to be set to 10. We prefer the expected number of ELSs to also be set to 10. But it is not unsual to use 20, 30, 50, or even on occasion 100.

If we were running formal protocols, we would have to penalize the p-values either in an internal manner or externally by the Bonferroni inequality. However, we do not do that here in our informal work.

The requirements that all ELSs be low skip rank ELSs which is what the expected number setting accomplishes, is actually not consistent with the form of the Torah code hypothesis that we hold: that only one or more of the ELSs, particularly the dominant ELS, must be low skip rank.

Thus, for now, we regard the setting of the expected number of ELSs to be a nuisance parameter.

We believe that when we understand the phenomena better, we will have a protocol that will know how to set it or how to work with various settings automatically and computationally efficiently.

Code Finder: Scores or Probabilities

Professor Robert M. Haralick Computer Science.Graduate Center City University of New York 365 Fifth Avenue New York, NY 10016"

Chapter Eight

A N C I E N T S E C R E T O F F I R S T

T O R A H C O D E S

D E C O D E S T H E P P R E S I C E

BIRTH TIME OF THE MOON WHICH IS THE FIRST ELS

The earliest written reference to equidistant letter sequences is in a comment made by RabbeinuBachya[25].

Rabbeinu Bachya lived in Spain in the mid thirteenth century. In his discussion of the first verse in Genesis he writes a cryptic footnote:

'**"If the eyes of your heart will be illuminated, you will find here precisely the code number that I mentioned above."**

It is encoded into the text in such a way that between each of its four letters lie 42 intervening letters.

The wise will understand that this not by chance, but a clear sign involving the very birth of the world.'

The footnote is with respect to a remark made in his commentary about four letters: בהרד.

What he means in this remark is that from the first ב of Genesis and skipping **42 letters)** 42 is the name of GOD Ana Bechach,aname connected with the name of GOD connected with the Creation of the World) there is a ה; and skipping 42 letters there is a רand skipping 42 letters there is a ד.

And he says this is the secret to the birth of the moon, lies in the birth of the world being a reference to the birth of the moon.

Day 2 Hour 5 204/1080 Hours	בהרד
Beginning	ראשית
Birth of	מלד
The Moon	הירח

This Torah codes table is showing the Hebrew letters בהרד as ELS with skip of 42 at the beginning of Genesis. The cylinder size is 42 and there also appears ELSs of the words: <u>Beginning Birth of the Moon</u>.

In the Jewish Oral Tradition, in an ancient book called **'Sod Halbbur'** it is written that the first new moon occured at hour 14 of day 6. The counting of the hours nominally begins at 6:00 PM the previous night, which is the beginning of the next day.

Hence, hour 14 of day 6 is 8:00 AM in the morning of day 6. The meaning of the בהרד can be understood by its Gematria.

Gematria: ב Pronounced **Bet** (= 2

ה (Pronounced **Hey'**) = 5

ר (Pronounced **Raish'**) = 200

ד (Pronounced 'Daalet') = 4

It means day 2, hour 5, plus 204/1080 parts of the hour.

In the Oral Jewish Tradition, it is taught that it arose in the mind of G-d one primordial year (12 lunar months) prior to Creation to create the world.

One lunar year prior to the first new moon occurred on day 2, hour 5 plus 204/1080 parts of the hour.

From this knowledge and knowing that the average length of the lunar cycle is just over 29.5 days, it is possible to compute the average length of the lunar cycle that has been taught in the Jewish Tradition from the time of Mount Sinai.

Here is how the calculation goes:

Multiply the truncated 29.5 days per lunar month by 12 to get 354 days per lunar year.

Since 350 is evenly divisible by 7, starting from day 2, hour 5 plus 204/1080 parts of the hour and going for 350 days brings us to day 2, hour 5 plus 204/1080 parts of the hour.

From day 2, hour 5 plus 204/1080 parts of the hour to day 6 hour 14 is 4 days, 8.8111 hours, or 4.3671296 days. One lunar year is then 354.3671296 days.

Divide this by 12 and we obtain the length of the lunar cycle as taught in the Jewish Oral Tradition since the time of Mount Sinai: 354.3671296/12 = 29.530594.

Of all the ancient cultures, which general held the lunar cycle to be 29.53 days. The 29.530594 days was most accurate.

NASA in 1996 by satellite observations plugged into celestial mechanics mathematics improved this to 29.530588 days.

The difference between 29.53094 days and 29.530588 days is about .5 seconds.

Chapter Nine

The first documented reference to equal distant letter skips is by **Rabbi Bachya ben Asher**(1255-1340). He writes of a 4 letter 42 letter skip **Equidistant Letter Sequence** (ELS) beginning from the first letter of the Torah that relates to the average length of the lunar month.

For a complete explanation of how this 4 letter ELS produces an amazingly accurate average length of the lunar month, see the discussion on *The First ELS*.

Rabbi Moshe Cordovero, as an acronym called 'The Ramak' (1522-1570) served as the Head of the Rabbinical Court ('Av Beit Din') in Tzfat, Israel, during the 16th century.

This was a time when Tzfat stood as the worldwide center for Jewish scholarship.

His book, *Pardes Rimonim*'is a voluminous commentary on the Zohar.

He writes in the introduction to Gate 30 that there are several ways that there is hidden information encoded in the Torah.

The secrets of our holy Torah are revealed through knowledge of: Combinations, Numerology

(Gematria), Switching letters, first-and-last letters Shapes of letters, First – and last – verses, **Skipping of letters דילוגי אותיות** - and **Eliyahu Rips מתתיהו, Matityahu Glazerson**.letter combinations.

These matters are powerful, hidden and enormous secrets.

Because of their great hiddenness, we do not have the ability to fully comprehend them.

Further, to see different angles through these methods is infinite and without limit. On this the Torah says, 'Its measure is longer than the world.

It was the cryptic comment by Rabbi Bachya that influenced **Rabbi Michael Dov Weissmandl** to engage in his study of the Torah Codes.

Rabbi Weissmandl was the Slovakian Rabbi who developed a smuggling operation near the Slovak - Polish border, which enabled thousands of Jews, at an high ransom price, to reach then therealtively safe Slovakia or Hungary.

Then Germany invaded Hungary and deportations began in the spring of 1942.

After 60,000 Jewish people had been sent to Auschwitz, Rabbi Weissmandl succeeded in negotiating with Dieter Wisliceny, the assistant to Adolf Eichmann, and was able with a $ 50,000 bribe to halt further deportations. Unfortunately, the deportations were only delayed.

Rabbi Weissmandl was fascinated by Rabbi Bachyas's cryptic comment on the 4 letter ELS. <u>He was certain that there was within the Torah, coded in equidistant letter sequences, divinely ordained information.</u>

He wrote out on white cards 10 x 10 arrays of the entire 304805 letters of the Torah and studied it for ELSs that were near multiples of 10.

After his death in 1957 his Talmud study students edited their notes of Rabbi Weissmandl' teachings, including some of his Torah codes and published the book called, ***Torat Chemed'***.

In 1976, Rabbi Shmuel Yaniv began working on equidistant letter sequences and associated Gematrias, specifically with respect to religious themes. And he began to incorporate this code point of view in his religious lectures.

Rabbi   Yaniv   published   his   first   book**צפונות בתורה**,*TzefunotBa'Torah*,Volume 1, in 1988, his second book with the title **צפונות בתורה**,*Tzefunot Ba'Torah*, Volume 2 in 1989, and his third book with the title **צפונות בתורה**, *TzefunotBa'Torah*, Volume 3 & 4 in 1990.

All his books are in Hebrew.

The translation of the title of Rabbi Yaniv]s'four -volume book series is, *Hidden Things in the Torah'*.

It was Rabbi Yaniv' teachings in the late 1970'that influenced **Professor Eliyahu Rips** to examine the Torah from the point of view of codes.

It was also Rabbi Yaniv who told Professor Rips about the existence of Rabbi Weissmandls book *Torat Chemed*.

The students of Rabbi Weissmandl wrote in the book that they do not remember some of the findings that Rabbi Weissmandl told them about.

For example, they did not know where the exact location of the ELS in the Torah with a skip of -50 at the end of the Book of Numbers was.

Later, but still in the early 1980'Professor Rips talked with **Doron Witztum** who had lived through 1979, in the same French Hill neighborhood as Professor Rips.

Witzum had been a PhD student at the Hebrew University studying and teaching physics.

He did his first degree in both Mathematics and Physics, specializing in General Relativity.

He left his physics studies in 1977 to devote his full time to Torah study.

In the spring of 1985 Witztum decided to do some research of his own about Torah codes.

Professor Rips gave him a program for searching for ELSs and this enabled him to do his work on the computers at the Jerusalem College of Technology.

In the Spring of 1985 Witztum had results he thought to be interesting and shared them with Professor Rips.

Witztum and Rips tell that they realized that the Torah Code phenomena occurred with those ELSs that are minimal on large portions of the text, including even ELSs with very big skips, and excluding short skip ELSs which are minimal skip ELSs on only short portions of the text.

This came to be known as **The Principle of Minimal Skips'**:

The better ELSs are those which are closer, in rank, to being minimal skip ELSs, even if their skips were large in absolute magnitude.

Witztum suggested focusing on ELSs that are minimal skip ELSs on large portions of the text and examine them for two kinds of patterns:

Meetings between minimal skip ELSs of one expression with a conceptually related expression in the string of letters of the Torah text itself meeting between: Near minimal skip ELSs of two conceptually related expressions.

It was at this meeting that Witztum suggested that the proximity of the two patterns should be measured on two-dimensional arrays.

Specifically, for a given ELS with skip *s* to consider cylinders with circumference *s, s/2, s/3* etc.

Witztum called this:

'The Principle of Two - Dimensional Writing' and it is on such code cylinders that all Torah code tables are shown till date.

Witztum called this 'The Principle of Two - Dimensional Writing', his ideas were immensely fruitful.

During the year 1985 through the year 1987, Doron Witztum produced a stream of remarkable findings.Professor Rips was particularly impressed with Witztums'discovery of the:הגאון מוילנא'The Gaon of Vilna'code, ('The Genius of Vilna'code).

The minimal skips for both key words in the book of Genesis have a remarkable meeting in a segment of only 46 letters out of 78064 letters of the book of Genesis.

This meeting is shown in the table below.

The Gaon	חגאון	From Vilna	מוילנא

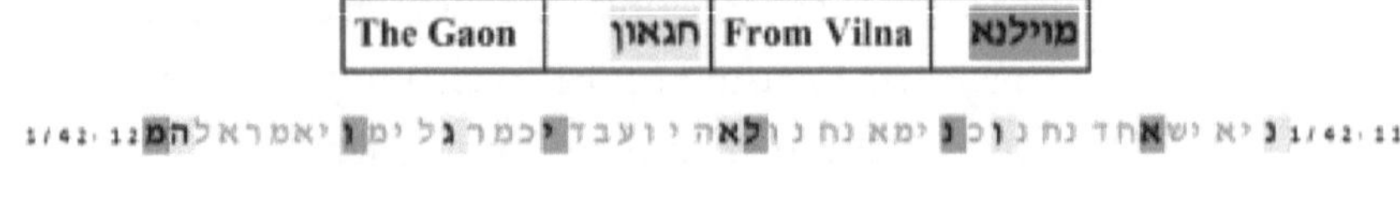

1

This is remarkable, **'The Gaon of Vilna'** table discovered by With expected number of ELSs set to 20, the probability that a text in the ELS random placement text population of the Five Books of Moses would produce a table as small or smaller than this one is 70.5/10,000.
WITZTUM'S

---

1.   http://torahcode.us/torah_codes/code_history/gaon_mvilna.png

F R E N C H R E V O L U T I N S T U D Y

French Revolution Study Through Torah Codes

One of Witztum'is early studies wasabout the French Revolution, an important historical topic.

In a time of three years, the royal monarchy that had ruled France for hundreds of years collapsed.

In some sense this was the beginning of an era of equal rights for all men in Europe.

The first table by Witztum that we show regarding this event has the keywords,**מהפכה הצרפתית** ('The French Revolution') And, **הצרפתית**('The French'),has only one ELS in the Book of Genesis and it is therefore the minimal ELS skip.

French	הצרפתית	Revolution	מהפכה

```
1/40·08  ובמשמרביתאדניולאמרמדועפנייכמרעימהיומול  1/40·07
1/41·25  ימואינמגידליויאמריוספאלפרעההחלומפרעהאח  1/41·24
1/42·09  יכריוספאתההחלווהמלאהכרהוויזכריוספאתהחל  1/42·08
1/43·09  נמאתהגמטפנואנכיאערבנומידיתבקשנואמלאקב  1/43·08
1/44·12  תאמתתתוארצהויפתחואישאמתתתוולחפשבגדולה  1/44·11
1/45·18  לכובאוארצהכנענוקחואתבתיכמובאו  1/45·17
1/46·34  הביאוהיהכייקראלכמפרעהואמרמהמעשיכמואמ  1/46·32
```

2

The cylinder size is 2103. This is the smallest area table having ELSs in Genesis of these key words.

The second table below shows the words meeting,Witztum found in Genesis with the smallest skip ELS for the key word,**בצרפת**,(InFrance') and the key word **מהפכה** , (Revolution') .

The second table below shows the meeting of words Witztum found in the Book of Genesis, with the smallest skip.

---

2.   http://torahcode.us/torah_codes/code_history/french_revolution1.png

Revolution	מהפכה	In France	בצרפת

(right)	letters (read right→left)	(left)
1/46·01	יויצחקויאמראלהימלישראלבמראתהלילהויאמר	1/46·02
1/46·03	קבמבארשבעוישאובניישראלאתיעקבאביהמואתט	1/46·05
1/46·07	לזרעוהביאאתומצרימהואלהשמותבניישראלהבא	1/46·08
1/46·12	נייהודהערואונןושלהופרצוזרחוימתערואונ	1/46·12
1/46·15	בנותיושלשימובנישלשובניגדצפיונוחגישוניואצ	1/46·16
1/46·19	לאשתיעקביוספובנימנויולדליוספבארצמצרימ	1/46·20
1/46·23	נידנחשימובנינפתלייחצאלוגוניויצרושלמאל	1/46·23
1/46·27	פששנימכלהנפשלביתיעקבהבאהמצרימהשבעימוא	1/46·28
1/46·30	ראלאליוספאמותההפעמאחריראותיאתפניככיעו	1/46·30
1/46·32	הביאןוהיהכייקראלכמפרעהואמרמהמעשיכמואמ	1/46·34
1/47·01	לאשרלהמבאומארצכנעןוזהנמבארצגשנומקצהאח	1/47·02
1/47·04	אשרלעבדיככיכבדהרעבבארצכנעןועתהישבונאע	1/47·04
1/47·06	ימקנהעלאשרליוויבאיוספאתיעקבאביוויעמדהו	1/47·07
1/47·09	נחייאבתיבימימגוריהמויברכיעקבאתפרעהויצא	1/47·10
1/47·13	לחמאינבכלהארצכיכבדהרעבמאדותלההארצמצרימ	1/47·13
1/47·15	מצרימאליוספלאמרהבהלנולחמולמהנמותנגדככ	1/47·15
1/47·17	בכלמקנהמבשנהההואותמהשנהההואויבאואליו	1/47·18

3

The cylinder size is 162. This is the smallest area for a table having ELSs in the Book of Genesis with these key words.

The **Storming of the Bastille** (French[4]: *Prise de la Bastille* [pʁizdə la bastij][5]) occurred in Paris[6], France[7], on the afternoon of 14 July 1789.

The medieval armory[8], fortress[9], and political prison[10] known as the Bastille[11] represented royal authority in the centre of Paris. The prison contained only seven inmates at the time of its storming but was seen by the revolutionaries as a symbol of the monarchy's abuse of power; its fall was the flashpoint[12] of the French Revolution[13].

In France, *le quatorze juillet* (14 July) is the National Day, usually called Bastille Day[14] in English.

---

3.   http://torahcode.us/torah_codes/code_history/french_revolution2.png

4.   https://en.wikipedia.org/wiki/French_language

5.   https://en.wikipedia.org/wiki/Help:IPA/French

6.   https://en.wikipedia.org/wiki/Paris

7.   https://en.wikipedia.org/wiki/France

8.   https://en.wikipedia.org/wiki/Arsenal

9.   https://en.wikipedia.org/wiki/Fortress

10.   https://en.wikipedia.org/wiki/Political_prisoner

11.   https://en.wikipedia.org/wiki/Bastille

12.   https://en.wikipedia.org/wiki/Flashpoint_(politics)

13.   https://en.wikipedia.org/wiki/French_Revolution

14.   https://en.wikipedia.org/wiki/Bastille_Day

S T O R M I N G O F T H E B A S T I L L E

The flashpoint of the French Revolution was on July 14, 1789 when mobs stormed the Bastille which represented the royal authority (Absolutism)in the center of Paris.

While the prison only contained 7 inmates at the time of its storming, its fall became an icon for the French Revolution.

The table below shows the closest meeting between ELSs in the Book of Genesis of the key words '**Bastille**' and '**Revolution**'Notice that the ELS for מהפכה ('Revolution') in this table and the previous two tables have the same skip of 9 ELS.

This ELS tightly links together these three tables, tables that appear on quite different and non-resonant cylinder sizes.

Bastille	בסטיליא	Revolution	מהפכה

```
1/39·02  ח ו י ה י [ב] ב י ת א ד נ י ו ה מ צ ר י ן י ר א א ד נ י ו כ י י ה ו ה א ת ו  1/39·03
1/40·11  כ ה ת א ו [ס] ו כ ל ע פ פ ר ע ה ו י א מ ר ל ו י ו ס פ ז ה ה פ ת ר נ ו ש ל ש ת ה  1/40·12
1/41·22  ת א ל מ ו [ט] ב ו ת ו ה נ ה ש ב ע ש ב ל י מ צ נ מ ו ת ד ק ו ת ש ד פ ו ת ק ד  1/41·23
1/41·56  צ ר י מ ו [י] ח ז ק ה ר ע ב ב א ר צ מ ו כ ל ה א ר צ ב א ו מ צ ר י מ  1/41·57
1/42·34  ד ע ה כ י [ל] א מ ר ג ל י מ א ת מ א ת ח י כ מ א ת נ ל כ  1/42·34
1/43·24  ר י ה מ ו [י] כ ו נ ו א ת ה מ נ ח ה ע ד ב ו א י ו ס פ ב צ ה ר י מ כ י ש מ ע  1/43·25
1/44·24  ע ל י נ ו [א] ו נ ו ע ב ד כ א ב ד ל ו א ת ד ב ר י א ד נ י ן י א מ ר א ב  1/44·25
1/45·23  ל ח מ ו מ ז ו נ ל א ב י ו ו י ל כ ו ו י ל ד ר כ ו י ש ל ח א ת א ח י ו ו י ל כ ו  1/45·24
1/46·32  ה ב י א ו ה ו י ה י כ ב מ ר ע ה א מ ר [פ] ה מ ע ש י כ מ ו א [ם] ל כ י ק ר א ל כ מ  1/46·34
```

15

The cylinder size is 1768. This is the smallest area within a table containing ELSs in the Book of Genesis with these key words.

At the time of the French Revolution the king of France was Louis XVI. He was from the Royal family of the House of Bourbon.

The table below, which Witztum discovered, shows the smallest area in a table in the Book of Genesis, containing the ELSs of the words '**House of Bourbon**' and '**Louis**'.

---

15. http://torahcode.us/torah_codes/code_history/bastille_revolution.png

House Of Bourbon	בית בורבון
Louis	לאוי

The cylinder size is 75. This is the smallest area with a table having ELSs in the Book of Genesis with these key words.

The table below presents the smallest table area having ELSs of the key words **'King Louis of France'**. He would be the last king of France and suffered the guillotine in 1793.

Louis	לואי
King	בצרפת
Of France	המלך

The cylinder size is 647. This is the smallest area within a table having ELSs in the book of Genesis of these key words.

By the late 1980' Witztum compiled his findings in his first Torah Code book under the title **הנוסף המימד**, ('*The Additional Dimension*'), which was published in the winter of the year 1988.

---

16.   http://torahcode.us/torah_codes/code_history/bourbon_revolution.png

17.   http://torahcode.us/torah_codes/code_history/louis_king.png

Chapter Ten

In the summer of 1985, Doron Witztum together with Professor Eliyahu Rips and **Yoav Rosenberg** (Former deputy head and analyst for the Israeli Government (Ret. Co.)

Former head "Talpiot" Program, BA in Physics and athematics, PhD in Computer Science) decided to investigate convergences between ELSs of the names and appellations of famous rabbinical personalities with their birth - and death dates.

This research would constitute a formal study of the meetings between near minimal skip ELSs of two conceptually related expressions.

At that time Yoav Rosenberg was a student at the Jerusalem College of Technology. It was Rosenberg who wrote the program. He later went on to complete his PhD in Computer Science at the Hebrew University.

To meet the ends of this goal a list of personalities was prepared, using the *'Encyclopedia of Great Men in Israel'* for the basis of the list.

The list was to include only the most famous individuals, i.e. those whose entries consisted of at least three columns of text, and for whom dates of birth and or death dates were cited.

A list of names and appellations were prepared, following the professional guidelines, by **Professor Shlomo Havlin** before the experiment began. Professor Havlin was the then head of the Department of Bibliography and Librarianship at Bar Ilan University.

The rules of Orthography and the form of the Hebrew date were also established *a priori* by the linguist **Yaakov Orbach**(of Blessed Memory).

Measurements of the convergences indicated that there is an extraordinarily strong tendency for some of the appellations of the personalitities to converge with their associated dates.

WRR published their results in the Hebrew University report, in autumn of the year 1986, describing their research in detail.

The report was also sent for review to **Professor Persi Diaconis**, who is a Statistician.

Thinking that the experimental results were due to tuning the method to the data, he proposed that a new list of famous personalities be prepared, to be investigated using the exact same program.

To compile the new list WRR took those personalities whose entries in the *Encyclopedia of Great Men of Israel* were between 1.5 and 3 columns of text, and for whom a date of birth and or death were cited.

These dates were written in the same format as previously established.

This time too, the list of names and appellations was prepared *a priori* by Professor Havlin, using the same professional criteria. Measurements were made using the same program as in the first experiment. The results were highly successful.

A paper describing the two experiments was published as a Hebrew University report in the winter of 1988. A shortened version of this paper was submitted for publication in the peer - reviewed multidisciplinary scientific journal, *Proceedings of the National Academy of Sciences*' by **Professor Robert Aumann**.

Professor Persi Diaconis was one of the reviewers. In a letter to Professor Robert Aumann, dated August 3rd, 1988, Professor Diaconis suggested that a permuation test be used to estimate the p-value of results.

Eventually the details of the test such as number of permutations and the requisite level of significance were agreed upon by Professor Diaconis and Professor Aumann, as laid out in a letter, dated

September 7th 1990, written by Professor Aumann and approved by Professor Diaconis two days later.

Professor Aumann delivered a copy of the agreement to WRR. By Professor Aumann'recommendation a new paper was composed, even before the experiment was run.

This version described the new test, leaving out the results, which did not exist yet. This paper was then sent to Professor Diaconis and to several other wellknown statisticians.

They approved the test (each one independently) as it was described in the paper and they stipulated the level of significance that should be required.

The experiment was run in the winter of 1991. The results were very significant: **P-value = 0.000016** Well beyond the proposed cutoffs.

The results were then incoroporated into the paper, which was finally published in the peer-reviewed Journal '*Statistical Science*', Vol. 9 (1994), No.3, 429-438.

The article in the journal indicates the affiliation of both Witztum and Rosenberg at the Jerusalem College of Technology.

The affiliation was brought to attention because Jerusalem College of Technology gave Witzum and Rosenberg access to their computation facility in return for a mutual agreement to list their affiliations as the Jerusalem College of Technology.

The method designed by Doron Witzum and Professor Eliyahu Rips regarding 'The Great Rabbi's Study' is interesting for scoring compactness.

This involved two independent components.

The first component was the compactness of pairs of ELSs in terms of their geometry on the cylinder.

The second component involved the quality of the ELSs. The quality of ELSs itself had two components.

The first component was the fraction of the text over which the ELS is minimal.

The second component was that in searching for ELSs, the maximum absolute skip was set so that the expected number of ELSs for the key word would be about 10.

In later years, Torah Code researchers such as Professor Robert Haralick did not fully appreciate the need for incorporating the quality of the ELS in terms of the fraction of the text over which the ELS was minimal or in terms of an ELS quality measure like the Rotenberg R-value.

At this stage, all tables of their research have been created using a protocol that utilizes the area of the table the compactness for the geometry component and the maximum absolute skip being set based on expected number of ELSs.

The resulting compactness measure is undoubtedly a less sensitive dectector than the original Witzum& Rips design.

T O R A H C O D E S O P P O N E N T S

"As iron sharpens iron, so one man sharpens another". Proverbs 27:17

The Torah Codes opponents not only systematically maligned Doron Witztum and Professor Eliyah Rips as if they were corrupt politicians, but also carried on an agenda of doing methodologically incorrect *non-apriori* experiments to show that compact tables can be found not only in the Torah but in non-Torah books as well. Indeed, counterfeit experiments produce counterfeit results.

This whole controversy from the counterfeit side, cased in a language that has the appearance of mathematical and statistical correctness can be found on the website of Professor Brendan McKay and friends.

And in the writings of Dr. Dave Thomas in the '*Skeptical Inquirer*', as well as on the former website of Professor Simon and that of Statistician Avraham Hasofer (Bless His Memory) .

In addition, you can review the slides by Professor Simon' talk against the Torah codes here:

http://torahcode.us/torah_codes/code_history/laslides/laslide1.htm

Following the publication of the paper in the Journal *Statistical Science,* in March 1994, Professor Rips was invited to give a guest lecture to the Israeli National Academy of Sciences on the subject of: *ELS' in the Book of Genesis – The Statistical Significance of the Phenomenon.*

A paper (in the Hebrew language) with the same title, co-authored by WRR, was submitted to INAS but was not published.

In 1995 WRR published as a reprint an article entitled: ***Equidistant Letter Sequences in the Book of Genesis: II. The Relationship to the Text.***

This article dealt with convergences between expressions appearing as ELSs and expressions appearing in consecutive letters in the Book of Genesis. One of the samples discussed in the article was the Nations Sample.

Measurements conducted on this sample indicated a particularly high level of statistical significance: The p-level for one of the two statistics used, was better than 4/1,000,000,000.

Considering critisms leveled against the composition of this sample and its measurement, by ProfessorDror Bar Natan, Professor Brandon McKay and ProfessorShlomo Sternberg.

A new and refined study was conducted which let to the p-value of 5/ 100,000,000,000.

Thus, a careful analysis of the critics'data and suggestions led to new results supporting the WRR research hypothesis with high significance.

Since WRRs' experiment using the second list, other experiments involving different lists have been conducted, including several designed to replicate the original second list experiment.

A few works and published papers are to be found on the website of Doron Witztum,

At the beginning of 1999, several lists of names and appellations were compiled by **Dr. Simcha Emanuel**, a specialist in Rabbinical History at the Tel-Aviv University.

He was engaged by MBBK (An acronym for 'McKay, Bar-Natan, Bar-Hillel &Kalai'), opponents of the Codes'research, Dr. Emanuels'was guided with his work by them without WRRs'knowledge.

One of the lists was intended to mimic" WRRs' second list.Emanuels'new list contains names and appellations of the personalities included in WRR'second list, which he collected without seeing Professor Havlins'original names and appellations for it.

Witztum repeated WRRs'original experiment exactly, with one single change: Instead of Havlins' names and appellations, he used Emanuels'. The experiment succeeded with considerable significance. One can read about it in the paper with the title:

'

New Statistical Evidence for a Genuine Code in Genesis',:

In 2004, Witztum published his second book צופן בראשית, To English, '*The Code of Genesis*', which describes and explains his research and gives an accurate account of the Torah Code phenomenon.

It furthermore documents the complete story of the WRR publication in the Journal *Statistical Science*.

Doron Witztum published a paper called, *The Hidden Birth Dates of Personalities of Genesis*, International Conference of Pattern Recognition.

If statistical analysis of many comparable texts show that there is a very low probability of these words appearing together in such a short passage, we may conclude that their appearance together in the Torah is not by chance but is an intentional encoded message.

MICHELSON, GANS AND SPIELBERG

"As iron sharpens iron, so one man sharpens another
Proverbs 27: 17

Professor Daniel Michelson became interested in Torah codes in the early 1980's after Professor Rips showed him his Torah code work. Dr. Michelson wrote a paper, see link:

Regarding codes, which was widely circulated in form of emails and which appeared in the publication Beor Ha Torah'in 1987.

His body of work brought knowledge regarding Torah codes to many people.

In the late 1980's, **Harold Gans**, then a Senior Cryptologic Mathematician (A Code Breaker') working for the National Security Agency, U.S. Department of Defense, heard about the Witztum, Rips and Rosenberg study (WRR) and found it hard to believe.In 1990, he undertookan independent evaluation, writing his own software that implemented a protocol almost identical to that of WRR.

He obtained nearly the same remarkable results of the association between rabbinic appellations and dates of their birth or death.

He then made an independent experiment pairing appellation of The Great Rabbis'Study'used in WRR with the cities of their birth or death.

He used a rule-based protocol developed by ZviInbal to provide the Hebrew transliteration of the Jewish names of the cities, (Meaning the names of the cities as they were called by Jews), that were required for the experiment. His results were even more significant than the WRR experiment.

The p-value was 1/166,000.

Some people raised questions about Inbals' rule-based protocol.

Gans then sought the expert opinions from rabbis literally all over the world, to check Inbal's rules.

Gans found, in fact that Inbals'ruleswas correct and he discovered as well that there was a name misprinted in one of the encyclopedia sources that they used.

Though to keep the protocol completely *a priori*, they did not correct the encyclopedia mistake in their city name data. Some years later Gans redid the experiment using the formula for measuring compactness as it was exactly used in WRR's studies.**The new p-value was 1/250,000.**

The paper describing the new experiment was given at the 2006 Pattern Recognition Conference.

Another scientist who became interested in the subject of Torah Codes in the 1980' was **Dr. Yochanan Spielberg**, who wrote his own program, called 'Bible Search Pro', which was commercially sold.

This is the programthat the Journalist **Michael Drosnin**, a Journalist of The Wall Street Journal and The Washington Post, and a Torah Codes researcher bought in 1992 and utilized to produce the tables in his first Torah Codes book, published 1997, a New York Times Bestseller, *The Bible Code*'.

According to Spielberg, he and Drosnin had a verbal agreement that Drosnin would credit Spielbergs' software in his book.

Drosnin never acknowledged that he used Spielbergs' software and in 2000 Spielberg initiated a lawsuit that was in 2001 ruled in Drosnins'favor. Spielbergs' website can be found at:.

Chapter Eleven

The encoded findings of biblical teachings in another dimension of Torahin 1991, during the time of war at the Persian Gulf region, Dr. **Alexander Rotenberg**immigrated to Israel and met Professor Rips, who told him about the Torah codes.

Which sparked Rotenberg'interest in Torah codes? He was so impressed by it that he decides to check it by himself. Together with a friend, **Andrey Smirnov** they worte the **Sof Sof Torah** program.

To date, this program remains one of the most vital tools for this research.They included in the SofSofTorah program the kind of statistical calculations Witztum, Rips and Rosenberg used in the WRR study, but created many other thoughtout useful functions designed by Dr. Rotenberg.

This is the main interactive program used by Professor Rips, even to this day. It is also the program of choice of Michael Drosnin for his research for his second and third Bible code book.

Dr. Rotenberg developed his own research protocol for the Torah Codes. It concentrates on closest word meetings and closest pairs of ELSs. He has compiled hundreds of examples showcasing their part in the foundation of encoding.

For an application of this principle, Dr. Rotenberg examined key words of some major Torah commentators as they wrote it down commenting on a Torah passage.

Rotenberg hypothesized that in or near these passages he would find ELSs of the exact same key words that the commentators used.In his book *And All this is Truth'* he summarizes many findings, which was published in 2005.

An example of that type of work is the finding that Dr. Rotenberg made within this table, which relates to the verse: ***And Nadav and Avihu died***, (Numbers 4:3.)

This is the story about the two sons of Aharon, who after the desert Temple, the so called Mishkan was sanctified took a strange fire into the Mishkan.

The Zohar (The weekly Torah portion Shemini) in commenting on the verse, '***Do not drink wine or strong drink, neither you, nor your sons with you.***'(Vayikra10:8) quotes Rabbi Yehuda.

Rabbi Yehuda said that from this chapter we learn that Nadav and Avihu were under the influence of wine by the very fact that the priests were warned about it.

Dr. Rotenberg found two sets of ELSs, one with '***Intoxicated with wine***' that cross the verse '***And Nadav and Avihu died***'. This is shown in the table below.

And died	וימת	Intoxicated	שתויי שתויי
Nadav	נדב	With Wine	יין יין יין
And Avihu	ואביהוא		

4/02·28	אמשמא וחמשמפ ימאלע וארבע ד	4/02·28
4/02·32	יתא ישראללב בני י וד ק	4/02·32
4/02·34	ישל וא נס ע וכ יהמנ גל ד	4/02·34
4/03·03	וא יה ואב ונדב וימת ן כה	4/03·03
4/03·06	ואתמשמרת ושמר ו ואת	4/03·06
4/03·09	ואת נ ואתאהר ישראל נ י	4/03·09	1

The ELSfor'**Intoxicated**' are long skip ELSs. The cylinder size is 150. With an expected number of ELSs set to 300, the probability that a text from the ELS random placement text population would produce a table with one set of ELSs of '***Intoxicated with wine***' crossing one of the two instances of '***And Nadav and Avihu died***' is less than **1/10,000**.

1.　　http://torahcode.us/torah_codes/code_history/nadav_avihu.png

In the early 1990's Dr. Moshe Katz worked on his own Torah code program and began giving talks on his Torah code research.

Dr. Katz was the first person to find the ELS of **Yitzchak Rabin'**name associated with the nearby key words: *Assassin will assassinate'*.

Dr. Katz communicated this information to Yitzchak Rabin's office, as well as to the people responsible for his security.

His main findings of that time period are published in his book called **Computorah'**, published in 1996 and comes together with his software.

In the early 1990'**Rabbi Matityahu Glazerson** and **Professor Robert Haralick** began working on Torah codes. They published their first book about Torah Codes in 1996. The title of the book, *Torah Codes and Israel Today'*.

The book is noteworthy because it formalized a different protocol than the one used for the WRR Torah code research study.

It associates with every Torah code table a measure of compactness, which is the length of the shortest length text segment that contained ELSs of each *a priori*specified key word.

It also measures the statistical significance of that shortest length text segment by performing the identical search in a randomly perturbed Torah text. The perturbation test favored in that book is the ELS random placement permutation method.

Professor Robert Haralick presented two papers at the 2006 International Conference on Pattern Recognition.

During this time, Torah code research results were often shown as tables which were rectangular windows extracted from the cylinder on which the table was found.Haralick'shortest length text segment was a linear measure of compactness which penalized tables found on large cylinder sizes.ProfessorRips'intuition was that this was not a good measure.

Therefore, Professor Haralick wrote new programs to use the area of the smallest table area that contained at least one ELS of each of the key words as a measure of compactness.

Dr. Jeffrey Satinover, a writer on controversial topics, became interested in the subject of Torah codes in the mid 1990's and published his book in 1997 called, *Cracking the Bible Code'*.

The book has a lot of information on the 'Torah Codes' history, as well as about Rabbi Weissmandl and the Holocaust.

Michael Drosnin, the New York Times best-selling author as mentioned prior got tremendous credit for making Torah codes widely known and popular.

In his book Drosnin tells the reader about his meetings with states leaders and the Torah code tables he shared with them. He also tells about how he interpreted the Torah codes tables to make predictions of the future.

Michael Drosnin was the second person who found ELS of Prime Minister Yitzchak Rabin, with the associated key words: *Assassin will assassinate'*, a year before the Rabin assassination.

Michael Drosnin frequently interacts and consults with Professor Eliyahu Rips. While he was writing his books, he frequently requested Professor Rips to review his tables, see if he saw anything else in the tables, or give his opinion about an interpretation of the tables he found himself.

Therefore, it is no wonder that there are about 70 pages of his book 'The Bible Code' in which the name 'Rips' is at least mentioned one time. On others, the name 'Rips' appears multiple times. Nevertheless, as we shall see from the upcoming statement, Professor Rips disassociates himself from the book.

Professor Rips made the following statement: While I did meet and talk to Mr. Drosnin, I did not do joint work with him. I do not support Mr. Drosnin's work on the Codes, nor the conclusions he derives.

There is an impression that I was involved in finding the code relating to Prime Minister Rabin' assassination.

This is not true. However, I did witness, in 1994, Mr. Drosnin find [ing of] the tableaux about Prime Minister Rabin, which now appears on the cover of his book.

It is the inference of predictions from what appears to be compact tables, exactly the kind of use of Torah code that Drosnin makes, that is particularly troubling to Torah code researchers. The making of predictions has a logical as well as statistical problem.

What was the basis of Drosnins'predictions? He had an initial hypothesis that he found a relatively compact table, one that in some intuitive sense was unlikely to occur by chance, and if the table had key words that described some future possible event, then the table was predicting the event would occur.

There are a few of these predictions that Drosnin would argue in fact happened.

There are others which did not. As these events did not occur, he had to revise his hypothesis: that the relatively compact table was only indicating the possibiblity of the event.

Of course the possibility that something might happen is not really any prediction at all, but in 1997 when the book was published, it was a good advertising to get people to buy his book which predicted disasters and catastrophies in 2000 and 2006 that did not occur. Disasters sell. Indeed, people did buy his book.

According to the Torah code hypothesis, if a major event happens, then some descriptive key words of the event is likely to have an associated relatively compact table in the Torah.

However, relatively compact tables from the Torah text do not mean anything because there are many relatively compact tables that do not correspond to any event.

Only if relatively compact tables had a one to one correspondence with events, could the finding of a relatively compact table be used for prediction.

This point, that a major event happening implies a relatively compact table, but a relatively compact table does not imply a majorevent is hard for many people to understand.

It is not unusual for people untrained in logic to make arguments and mistake the A *implies* B proposition as equivalent to the B *implies* A proposition.

In short, there exist compact tables having ELSs of key words describing an event, its time and place that never has happened or will happen.

And there is no way to distinguish the compact tables that do correspond to real events except by a proper experiment using *a priori* key words.

That many people do not understand this unfortunately clouds the proper understanding of Torah codes.

Now, let us read what Harold Gans and Doron Witztumexplicitly stated about Drosnin's book. Harold Gans, made this statement, 'The book states that the codes in the Torah can be used to predict future events. This is unfounded.

There is no scientific or mathematical basis for such a statement, and the reasoning used to come to such a conclusion in the book is logically flawed.

While it is true that some historical events have been shown to be encoded in the Book of Genesis in certain configurations, it is not true that every similar configuration of "encoded" words necessarily represents a potential historical event.

In fact, quite the opposite is true: most such configuarionts will be quite random and are expected to occur in any text of sufficient length.'DoronWitztum made the following statement'there is a danger that the entire credibility of codes research will be destroyed. Mr. Drosnins' work employs no scientific metholody.

No distinction is made between statistically valid codes, and accidental appearances, which can be found in any book.

For example, Drosnin "code" of th comet Shoemaker Levy crashing into Jupiter is statistically meaningless. Such a code can be found by accident in 1 out of any 3 books checked! Drosnin carries through his incorrect inference that Torah codes can be the basis of predictions in his second book *Bible Code II*, published in 2002, and his third book *Bible Code III*, published in 2010. In fact, on page 4 of his 2010 book he writes:

The Bible Code did not predict the obvious. Again, and again it predicted what no one believed possible and then it came true.

This kind of statement is unfortunate because it is easy to produce statistically significant tables based on the kind of topics, he has shown in which the key words, "predict," in his sense, something historically incorrect, totally incorrect.

This is the reason that proper Torah code experiments must have a protocol and the key words must be *a priori* key words.

On the more positive side, Drosnin is truly devoted to the Torah Codes.

He is serious and sincere in his attempts to discover and inform political leaders of potential disasters, by the interpretations he has of the tables he has found. His experimental protocol is not *a priori*.

His intuition about table compactness has has improved with time. Many of the tables in his third book, published in 2010 would indeed have high statistical significance, when evaluated according to standard protocols, assuming *a priori* key word lists.

As a side note, although Drosnin is a good popular writer, he evidently is not a trustworthy historian.

His 2010 book has some historical inaccuracies, crediting Professor Rips with discovering the Bible code (page 9), crediting Professor Rips with writing a codes computer program (page 9) and jointly writing a codes computer program with Dr. Rotenberg (page 205). We have spent more space discussing Drosnin than really intended.

But since Drosnin's books are popular, people may incorrectly think that it is methodologically correct to make predictions from Torah codes or people may realize that it is not methodologically correct and think that therefore all the serious work is also not methodologically correct.

Thus, Drosnin mistake spreads by association and reflects badly on all serious Torah code researchers. It is for this reason that good communicators must be held to a higher standard.'

Chapter Twelve.

The hidden location of The Ark of The Covenant in Torah Codes
In this section we provid a brief description of some of the people we know who are doing Torah codes research work or who have written about Torah codes research.

Michael Drosnin firstbest selling book, published in 1997 was influenced by a man named **Barry Roffman**, Roffmanis a researcher on the Torah codes and had a hypothesis that if anything is encoded, it certainly would be that the Ark of the Covenant and its location would be encoded.

As he began to develop tables, he saw the beginning characters of ELSs in the table as relating to the beginning characters of other ELSs as a course direction in a north, south, east, west sense.

He developed this hypothesis into the book,'*Ark Code*', published in 2004, in which he hypothesizes, based on these kinds of relationships, locations just off the Egyptian coast in the Mediteranean Sea where the Ark of the Covenant should be located.

The basis for Roffman's Torah codes work on the Ark of the Covenant are tables having the key word for Ark of the Covenant and Jerusalem plus names of places that satisfy a constraint which makes them interesting to Roffman.

There are two places just on the coast of Egypt that Roffman finds interesting.

They are Zuqba and Bardawal. The table below has all the four key words. From the ירושלם of, Jerusalem, to the **of** צקבה, Zuqba, it is 7 rows down and 22 columns across. A triangle with opposite side of 7 and base 22 has an angle whose tangent is 7/22 =.3182.The angle is the arc tagent of .3182 which is 17.65 degrees.

Starting from north, which he aligns with the top of the table, and rotating clockwise to 270 degrees less 17.65 degrees comes to 252.35 degrees.

Zuqba is interesting because the geographic course heading from Jerusalem to Zuqba is 252.35 degrees. A similar kind of reasoning indicates that Bardawal is interesting.

Ark of the Covenant	ארון ברית	Zuqba	צקב צקב
Jerusalem	ירושלם	Bardawil	ברדול

```
4/32·22   יה והעדה ור יש ואתא לב י ומפ נ י ו ו נכבשה הארצלפ נ י יה וה ואחרתש
4/32·27   חמה כאשראד נ י דבר ו י צ ו להממשה אתאלע זרהכה נ ואת יה וש עבנ נ ו ן
4/32·33   ומעברל ירד נ ו י ת נ להממשהלב נ י גד ולב נ י רא ו ב נ ולחצ יש בטמ נשהב
4/32·40   כ י רב נמ נשה גלעדה ו י לכדה ו י ורשאתהאמר יאשרבה ו י ת נמשהאתה ל
4/33·04   י שראל ב י דרמהלע י נ י כלמצר ימ ומצר ימ מקבר ימאתאש דהה כה יה וה בה
4/33·12   מ ו י סע ומא ילמ ו י ח נ ו על ימס ופ ו י סע ומ ימס ופ ו י ח נ ו במ דברס י נ ו
4/33·24   ובקהלתה ו י סע ומקהלתה ו י ח נ ובהרשפר ו י סע ומהרשפר ו י ח נ ובחרד
4/33·38   ח נ ובמדברצ נה ואקדש ו י ח נ ובהרההרבקצהארצאד ומ ו י
4/33·46   י סע ומע ימ ו י ח נ ובד י ב נ גד ו י סע ומד י ב נ גד ו י ח נ ובעלמ נדבלת ימ
4/33·53   תמתאבד ו ואתכלבמ ותמתשמ י ד ו וה ורשתמאתהארצ ו יש בתמבהכ ילכמ
4/34·02   מרצ ואתב נ י ישראל ואמרתאלהמכ יאתמבא ימאלהארצכ נע נ ו זאתהארצ
4/34·08   פ ו נמ נה ימה גד לתתא ולכמהרהההרמהרהרתתא ולבאחמת וה י ות וצאת
```

1

This is a table that shows that the heading from ELSs of Jerusalem to Zuqba of the table agrees with the geographic course heading.

Roffman uses the interactive Code Finder program which permits ELSs to wrap around the Torah. Mr. Roffman does not use the analytic calculation the Code Finder program makes to determine p-values.

Rather, he has developed his own way of doing an analytic calculation that approximates a p-value. His calculation is better than that in the Code Finder program.

Sometimes it is close, but it is not unusual for it to be off an order of magnitude.

The only proper way to estimate a p-value is by a Monte Carlo experiment and none of the commercially available software does that.More tables can be found on Barry Roffman website:

---

1.   http://torahcode.us/torah_codes/code_history/ark1.png

Art Levitt began exploring the Torah codes from about 1997, influenced by a Discovery Seminar; he has since worked with Professor Rips.

Levitt is a quite careful researcher, always employing proper protocols, and his p-value estimates are conservative,(meaning that the true p-values are much lower than his estimate).

He presented several papers at the 2006 International Conference on Pattern Recognition. His most recent study is with the application of the Divine Names in Torah codes. His website can be.

There are a few more individuals who have conducted research work in the field of Torah codes, not all of them are well known.

Nachum Bombach worked on researching Torah Codes from the mid 1990'Bombach and Gans presented a paper at the 2006 International Conference on Pattern Recognition.

They also went ahead and presented another paper with other researchers at the same conference.

Igor Pisetskiand**Chaim Stahl** worked on the Torah codes research from the the late 1990. lthough they have found many interesting tables, their work is unfortunately not published online.

Dr. Leib Schwartzman worked on the Torah codes research from the late 1990, He prefers to work with minimal skip ELSs and has developed the dialogue technique.

Boaz Metzger has worked with Professor Rips on the Torah codes research; his findings are available for review at: http://torah-codes.com[2] .

Another individual doing the Torah codes research is **Rabbi Matityahu Glazerson**. Rabbi Glazerson views the Torah codes as one of the official methods that should be applied to interpret the Torah, which for him falls under the same category as Gematria.

---

2. http://torah-codes.com/

He interprets each given table from the Torah point of view, letting the tables reinforce the teachings of Traditional Judaism.

This method is similar to studying the surfaces of a polished gem stone, even though one is looking at each surface from a different angle, expressing different prisms of light, they all belong to the same stone and reinforce the perception of the stone being one with different angle expressions.

Therefore, Rabbi Glazerson does develop the Torah codes tables always with context. The context are the verses found in the actual Torah, which are the tables to be found in the plain text, as well as the commentary of the Sages and the homiletic and esoteric interpretations of the Torah verses.

Therefore, Rabbi Glazersonis able to bring forth additional key words in his search, relating to the teachings of the Sages, as well as the Oral Teachings discussed in the Midrash[26] and in Kabbalah(the Zohar).

Due to his extensive knowledge of the Midrash, Rabbi Glazerson is often able to select key words for a topic, which is discussed in the Midrash and which relates to an historical event or a Torah concept.

From the mid 1990'he began using Torah codes tables to reinforce his lectures on Torah.

In 2001 he published the book, the Twin Towers in Torah Codes'. He, much like Professor Rips, utilizes the interactive Torah codes program called,'SofSof' designed by Rotenberg.

The Torah codes tables he has developed and published in the The Twin Towers in Torah Codes' book, entirely involve short skip ELSs which he shows in the actual text itself, without making special tables extracted as windows on a cylinder.

The Twin Towers Attack'cause decoded through Torah Codes and Kabbalistic teachings.

To illustrate the nature of Rabbi Glazerson table interpretation method, we consider a table about the 'Twin Towers' shown in the following table. The table includes the key words forming the sentence:

Twin TowersAttackwith AirplaneAgainstEdomFrom Islam.

Twin Towers	מגדלין התאומים	Against	נגד
Attack	מתקפת	Edom	אדום
With Airplane	במטוס	From Islam	מהאסלם

The cylinder size is 36. With expected number of ELSs set to 25, the probability that a text from the ELS random placement text population would have as small an area table as the one produced from the Torah text is less than 1/1,000,000.[3]

Regarding this table Rabbi Glazerson explains that the Gematria of: **Twins, התאומים** is 502.

This equals the Gematria of the metaphorical twins, which are: **Yishmael'ישמעאל**, which has the Gematria **451**.

' **Edom- אדום**, which has the Gematria **51**. (Yishmael) **451** + (Edom) **51** = **502**

---

3.   http://torahcode.us/torah_codes/code_history/twin_towers2.png

According to the Jewish Teachings Edom is the Kingdom of Christianity. Therefore, Edom is represented through Europe, the countries of the North American continent, Australia, and New Zealand.

The contemporary leading country of Edom is the United States. The Kingdom of Yishmael is according to the Jewish Teachings the Arab Nations and countries of the Middle East.

'Yishmael is encoded in the same text area but its ELS has the small skip of 11. In order to see it, we must use a smaller cylinder size. A table showing the ELS for 'Yishmael' is shown next.

Twin Towers	מגדלין התאומים
Yishmael	ישמעאל
From Islam	מהאסלם

The cylinder size is 12. With the expected number of ELSs set to 25, the probability that a text from the ELS random placement text population would have as small as of atable area as the one produced from the Torah text is 20/10,000.

The two Twin Towers tables shown above appear in the text spanning The Book of Numbers, Chapter 19, verse 11, through The Book of Numbers Chapter 20, verse 14.

The text material to be found of interest is in the Book of Numbers, Chapter 20 and begins with the death of Miriam.

And as the Midrash explains, there was a well called, Miriams' well.' As the Jews (Hebrews/ Israelites) were wandering through the wilderness, lacking adequate water supply would have been fatal.

In the merit of Miriam, G-d provided a moving well of water, one which virtually followed the people throughout their wanderings, until the moment of Miriam's death. When Miriam died, so did the well.

Thus, there was no more water. And therefore, the Israelites complained about the lack of water following Miriami passing.

G-d instructed Moses to take his staff and speak to the rock before the eyes of the Israelites and water gushed forth from the rock.

Moses took his staff and as it is stated in the Book of Numbers 20:11, *Moses* **raised his arm and struck the rock with his staff twice; abundant water came forth and the assembly and their animals drank.**

The original Hebrew text of this verse is to be found in a first table, about six rows from the bottom.

The symbolism of the 'rock', to Hebrew, **סלע**, that Moses struck, can be understood by words formed out of its Hebrewletters: **ס, ל, ע**

These words that can be formed out of them are all associated with the forces of evilthe first word begins with its first letter: **ס**Samech Which is the first letter of the name: **סמאל** 'Samael'.

Samael is the heavenly minister of the biblical character Esau

The principal characteristic of people that have internalized some spiritual similarity to Samael is HaughtinessThe second word begins with its second letter: **ל** (Lamet') which is the first letter of the name: 'Lilith' to Hebrew, **Lilith-לילית** is the wife of Samael. The biblical character associated with Lilith is **Hagar**, the mother of Yishmael.

The prinicipal characteristics of people who have internalized some spiritual similarity to Lilith is '**Desire,**' desire in the sense of lust.Hence, this is the established connection of Lilith to Yishmael.

The third word begins with its third letter:

ע (Eyin)which is the first letter for the word **Or** - עור its literally meaning to English, Skin'.

The skin represents the covering, the shell, in kabbalsitic terms called a Klipah, which is a covering/shell of impurity that joins that what it covers together with itself hiding its full purpose due to to sin. (That goes much in line with the famous saying, Knowledge is power.

According to Kabbalah to have this power sin has to be corrected, which then as a result removes the skin/klipah and therefore causes one to understand what is really going in life.

Given this analysis, it should be no surprise that both Samael and Lilith appear as ELSs in the same text area.

The ELS for Samael has a skip of 16 and that of Lilith has a skip of 67. Notice that the ELS for Samael begins with the letter samech for the Hebrew word for '**rock**'. These tables are shown next.

English	Hebrew
Twin Towers	מגדלין התאומים
Samael	סמאל
Skin	עור
From Islam	מהאסלם
Rock	סלע

The cylinder size is 18. With the expected number of ELSs set to 50, the probability that a text from the ELS random placement text population would have as small of a table area as the one produced from the Torah text is smaller than 1/ 100,000.

---

5.   http://torahcode.us/torah_codes/code_history/twin_towers4.png

Twin Towers	מגדלין התאומים
Lilit	לילית
From Islam	מהאסלם
Rock	סלע

The cylinder size is 36. With the expected number of ELSs set to 50, the probability that a text from the ELS random placement text population would have as small of a table area as the one produced from the Torah text is smaller than 1/10,000.

On September 11th, 2001, Osama Bin Laden, a Moslem and founder of the transnational extremist Salafist militant organization Al-Qaeda, attacked the Twin Towers. Bin Laden was being supported and sheltered by the Taliban, a Sunni Islamic fundamentalist political movement and military organizationgoverning in Afghanistan.

The quite four weeks after the attack, on the afternoon of October 7th, the US, Canada, the United Kingdom, and Australia, began airstrikes on the capital of Afghanistan, the airport of Kabul, at Kandahar, home of the Taliban's Supreme Leader Mullah Omar, and in the city of Jalalabad.

6.　http://torahcode.us/torah_codes/code_history/twin_towers5.png

The next day, October 8ᵗʰ was the seventh day of the Jewish Holiday called 'Sukkot' This day is called 'Hashana Raba', The Day of Final Judgement.

This is the day on which G-d seals the Book of Judgement for all Creation, finalizing and sealing the destiny of each person for the new year, based on their merits and sins from the last year)Each year mankind is judged again, not only once their lifetime is over, as many people assume).

And this is the day, which according to our Sages will mark the beginning of the war called,

Gog and Magog.

By writting out each letter in its full ronounciation(Which is an official and classic method of Gematria) we obtain the letters: [גימל] ואו מ גימל ואו גימל] [ואו גימלGimmel, Yud, Mem, LamedVav, Alef, VavGimmel, Yud, Mem, Lamed .

Magog: Vav, Alef, Vav Mem, Gimmel, Yud, Mem, Lamed, Vav, Alef, Vav Gimmel, Yud, Mem, Lamed

The Gematria of '**Gog and Magog**'written out to Hebrew is: 451, which equals the Gematria of the d Yishmael, ישמעאל.GematriaGog and Magog: **451.**

The fact that Gog and Magog is to be written out to have the same Gematria result shows, that Ishmael is the inner essence, the soul of the war of Gog and Magog.

Rabbi Glazerson teaches that the Zohar (Exodus (Portion)Vaera32:1), speaks of three wars that Yishmael will declare.

In the future, Yishmael will declare three fierce wars to the world and the descendants of Edom will gather against the descendants of

Yishmael and fight three battles. One battle will take place at the sea, one on land and one near Jerusalem.

Evidently, the attack on Afghanistan marked the beginning of the battle on land.

Rabbi Glazerson teaches that The World Trade Center The Twin Towers, was the quintessential financial center in the world, which housed gold and diamonds as well as had the largest offices.

As such some people (With many acceptions) involved in these financial trades, had a self awareness of being one of the most vital movers and shakers on the financial world stage and its towers became the symbolism of a developed arrogance in the world, which stems from a place of wisdom. Rabbi Glazerson notes that the Gematria of the word

Tower, מגדל, is 77 which equals the Gematria of the word '**Wisdom**', to Hebrew, חכמה plus its number of letters. (Which is a classic method of calculating Gematria).

As already discussed, the Gematria of The Towers' תאומים is **502**, which is also the Gematria of Yishmael plus Edom, since the Arrogance and lust' that the towers represented are the forces of Yishmael and Edom.

In 2004, Rabbi Glazeron published the book called '*The End of Darkness*', Hebrew title, קץ שם לחשך.

The book relates Torah codes from theperspective of Kabbalah. Which is considered in Kabbalah a tool of repentence, through decoding its meanings and therefore causing salvatin.

In 2005, Rabbi Glazerson published in conjunction with Professor Robert Haralick and Professor Eliyahu Rips the book called,'*Torah Codes: A glimpse Into the infinite*', a book that discusses technical and statistical protocol issues as well as answers various Torah codes critics.

The book also has a set of remarkable Torah codes tables about recent historical events.

In 2005, Rabbi Glazerson published the book, *The Tsunami in Skips (Torah Codes)*' titled,‫הצונאמי בדילוגים‬.

In 2006, Rabbi Glazerson published the book, *Yisrael – Yishmael*, abook full of tables relating to the Palestinian and Arab Leaders, all of whom wish to destroy Israel.

In the same year of 2006, Rabbi Glazerson published the book called *The Skips and the Hidden Light*', Hebrew title,‫האור הגנוז‬ ‫בדילוגים‬, which discusses the Jewish Holiday 'Chanukah' and Torah Codes that relate to this miraculous and devasting historic event and its spiritual meaning.

In 2008, Rabbi Glazerson along with Professor Robert Haralick continued working on the topic of the conflict between Hamas and Israel.

In 2008 Rabbi Glazerson published a book regarding the real root causes of the Holocaust, called, **The Holocaust in Torah Codes'**.

Most recently, he and Professor Robert Haralick published a book called, *The Mayan Culture and Judaism*,' which carriesas the topic of interpretations regarding the auspicious year '2012'. According to Kabbalah, 2012 is one of the auspicious candidate years for the arrival of the Messiah.

Furthermore, discussed in the book are the related concepts to the teachings of the Mayan culture and their mirroring views to Judaism. All the informations are supported by Torah codes tables' throughtout the book.

Rabbi Glazerson most recent book published in 2010 is called, *'Bible Codes and Kaballah'*. The book describes Torah codes as having an outer layer and inner layer.

The inner layer consists of the statistically unusual compact arrangements (tables) of historically and logically related key words. These words are found at significant equidistant letter sequences (ELSs) and appear in relevant portions of the text.

The deeper inner layer consists of the Torah interpretations and teachings related to these tables. These torah teachings are derived from the meaning of the Torah verses contained in the tables and the relationship between those relevant key words found in the tables.

The commentary is based on the Written and Oral Traditions given simultaneously at the revelation on Mount Sinai. Also demonstrated in the book are the standards for Torah code tablesandexpound upon protocols and statistics governing the kind of tables that constitutes Torah codes and of those who do not.

The reader can view a remarkable set of tables and explore the significance of the codes according to either the interpretations of the Torah verses that make up the table or by the Oral tradition that teaches the wisdom of the relationship of the key words to the pertinent sections of text and to one another.

In the late 1990's **Dr. Robert Wolf** and **Joe Gallis** became interested in the Torah Codes. They decided to use a protocol that concentrates on positive skip ELSs whose absolute skip is generally 100 or less.

The key words are pertinent to the Torah verses they are encoded within, and the interpretation of the Torah code is always with repsect to the Torah Tradition.

In 1999, Wolf and Gallis, published their book, *Between the Lines* and a second Volume with the same title was published in 2001.

In 2003, Wolf and Galls worked in conjunction with Rabbi Glazerson and Professor Haralick to publish the book called

'Light Out of Darkness – Surviving the End of Days'.

Wolf and Gallis show ELSs in the actual text of the Torah, rather than making tables. This has the adventageof not requiring resonance among the ELSs that is part of the study.

Its disadvantage on the other hand is due to not creating tables for the research, there are no statistical evaluations of their findings.

In their second book, *Between the Lines'* – Volume II, they discuss the impeachment of Bill Clinton.

The key word,**Clinton**'occurs as an ELS in the book of Genesis, Chapter. 34. The Chapter tells of an illicit sexual relationship between Shechem, a non-Jewish king, and Dinah, the daughter of Jacob.

The parallel between this scenario and what occurred with former President Clinton and Monica Lewinsky is striking.

In this section there is an ELS for the key word '*Impeachment*', Liar', and 'Adulterer'. The prosecutor was Kenneth Starr and the key word 'Starr' appears in the same section. This is shown in the following table.

Clinton	קלנטן	Adulterer	נאף
Impeachment	גנוי	Star	כוכב
Liar	משקר		

7

This table is not statistically significant. But the place in which it occurs in the Torah is related to the key words.

.

For those interested, scientific protocols for evaluating intelligibility of long ELS phrases can be found in the paper by Art Levitt, see link:http://www.torah-code.org/papers/belgpdf.pdf, et. al..

---

7.   http://torahcode.us/torah_codes/code_history/clinton.png

We may advice Mr. Sherman and Dr. Jacobi even though their intention might be noble, to validate their work, by following such a protocol.

Daniel Stochelbegan working on the Torah codes research in 1999, standing out is his work regarding the concept of the End of Days.

The Zohar comments that there is a place in Torah that contains the secrets of The End of Days.

This place is in the (Portion) of the Torah known by the name 'Veyechi'. It is located from Genesis 47:28 through Genesis 50:26.

The Zohar says that everything that will happen to the Jewish Nation in the End of Days is sealed and hidden in Veyechi.

Stochel table is actually a cluster of layered tables, each of which reveals colorful details about the End of Days given in the blessing of Yaakov (Jacob) to his twelve children.

The Matrix and all of its vast findings are released along with his book called, ***Until the Hour of Redemption'***.

Stochels'work publication timing falls elegantly into the time called according to Jewish Tradition The Final Days'.

His website contains all his tables but is currently not public.

Moshe Shak began working on Torah codes in about the year 2000.

His book ***Bible Codes Breakthrough- Amazing Matrices and How-To Guide'*** published in 2004, explains how anyone can do Bible code work, and then shows matrices developed using the stated protocols.

The interactive protocol explained in the book, was developed by Shak himself and contains many Torah codes tables. His interactive protocol begins with a minimal skip term and selects ELSs that have sufficiently large R-values and pays attention to redundancy

Andy McKracken has an extensive body of work about Torah codes, see his website: http://www.exodus-codes.com/.It also includes the work of many others, such as:

LyubenPiperov,

Fabrice Bect,

Jimmie Cash,

Jim Wright,

And Al Sutton.

Many of the tables that are appearing on McKracken's website contain key words that are not so clearly related to the main topic of the table. Some of the tables are relatively large, and certainly not compact.

McKracken and Jim Wright use the Bible software for their work of searching key words.

One of the researchers in the group, LyubenPiperov relates with his writing of Torah codes to a variety of topics; he thinks broadly and technically, using mathematics and probability derivations to support his conclusions. His most recent study is about symmetry.

A recent table by Piperov has the subject of a '**Scepter, -שבט**.

The septer is an extension of the hand and the arm. It is a symbol of rulership, protection, power and authority. In the Torah, the scepter held by Moses is an extension of Gods' hand and arm.

It is also the symbol for the power and authority that will be given by G-d to the Messiah.

Recall the verses in Genesis:

The scepter shall not depart from Judah, nor a lawgiver from between his feet, until Shiloh comes; and to Him shall be the obedience of the people.(Genesis49:10)

And in the prophecy of Baalam it says:I see Him, but not now; I behold Him, but not near; A Star shall come out of Jacob; a Scepter shall rise out of Israel. (Numbers24:17)

Piperov was particulary interested in the verse from Psalm 2, which qualifies the scepter with iron. There is the translation for 'Septer', שבט, is rod and the phrase is, 'Iron rod'.

You will smash them with an iron rod: you will shatter them like a potter's vessel. (Psalm 2:9)

Piperov writes, Therefore, it seemed interesting to check if there is any statistically significant occurrence of the key word שבט ברזל, iron rod, as an ELS. Surprisingly, the smallest greater than 1 skip occurs in the Book of Leviticus.

But what seems to be most amazing is that it intersects the very verse, where G-d has stated regulations Aaron should adhere to for the sin offering.

The procedur includes breaking the used earthen utensils or clay pots but sparing those made of copper.

An earthenware vessel in which it was cooked shall bebroken; but if it was cooked in a copper vessel, that should be purged and rinsed in water. (Leviticus6:21)'

And an earthenware vessel	וכלי חרש
Iron rod	שבט ברזל

The cylinder size is 37. The table spans from Leviticus 6:21 through Leviticus 7:3.

Remarkably, an ELS for the key word, 'Iron rod' occurs right in a section that discusses the breaking of earthenware vessels that had absorbed the taste of the sin offering and therefore became impure and had to be shattered.

Professor Robert Haralick gives the following interpretation of Mr. Piperov's table. 'They had to be shattered because the contamination of an earthenware vessel from impurity cannot be washed away with water.

To understand the relationship between the scepter of the Messiah and the breaking of the contaminated earthenware vessel, recall that G-d made mankind from the earth. So, earthenware vessel is a metaphor for people.

In the war of Gog and Magog, it is the iron rod of the Messiah who will break the impure earthenware vessels, meaning those people and nations who stand against G-d.

Shattering the impure earthenware vessels means obliterating from existence those who stand against G-d.

---

8.   http://torahcode.us/torah_codes/code_history/iron_rod.png

Chapter Thirteen

We have grouped the following researchers together because they all use **Kevin Acres'** Code Finder program and show the goodness of the tables, they construct in terms of the odds ratio that the Code Finder program calculates.

Roy Reinhold began working on Torah codes in about 2000. He is a promoter of the Code Finder Bible code program. His website contains a variety of Torah code tables as well as tutorials on codes and how to use the Code Finder program.

His website also hosts tables produced by other Torah code researchers. Mr. Reinhold has a hypothesis that what is encoded is encoded in clusters of compact tables that are nearby to each other.

The hypothesis is interesting and deserves to be formally stated and statistically tested.

Therefore, many of his tables are large with two or more clusters nearby to each other. His website can be foundat,http://ad2004.com/Biblecodes/index.html.

Fabrice Bect became interested in Torah codes in the late 1980' after reading about some of the results of Professor Eliyahu Rips and Doron Witztum.

Bect found particularly interesting the tables found by WRR, which are documented in their Hebrew University report and in the subsequent book by Doron Witztum.

An ELS of the key word **'Bastille'** occurs near an ELS of the key word for **'Revolution'**, referring to the French Revolution of 1789.This ELS for **'Bastille'** crosses the phrase from the surface text: *'The prison, a place where the king'sprisoners are held.'*

'**Bastille**' is a key word since the storming and fall of the Bastille was the flashing point of the French Revolution.

Moreover, around the axis term appear satellite words" that are related to the main term from the meaning point of view.

But this it not all, if one starts all over again, all the operation using another word whose meaning is the same as the first term, this second main term and its satellites appear in the same location as the satellites that appear in the same location as the preceding series. which means that the words with the same meaning are geometrically close to each other in the text of the Torah.

Bect has tables on several different websites, none of the websites contain all his tables contained in one website. Some tables can be found on McKracken's website and on others.

In addition to the Code Finder software, Bect also uses the ABD Pro software and sometimes 'The Keys to the Bible software.This is Bect's approach to find tables:

First, he selects the main key word and finds all the ELSs of that key word.

This key word is the axis key word. He begins with the smallest skip ELS of the axis key word. Then he continues to look and see if this ELS is nearby a word, or an expression, or a verse, or a text with a relating meaning.

Finally, by dividing the cylinder size by 2, 3, 4 etc. he looks for ELSs of other words that are relevant to the topic.

One of Mr. Bect's recent tables contains the key words, **Newton'** and '**Gravity**' and is shown next.

The *a priori* axis term is נ׳וטון, **Newton'**. The ELS for '**Newton**' in this table is the sixth smallest skip ELS of the name in the Torah.

The key wordsvnahfv,חוק המשיכה, **Gravitation Law'** are the other*a priori* key words. The key words חק עולם, which can be translated as, '**Eternal Law**' or**Law of the Universe**'occur as ELSs twice and is considered as a snooped term.

Newton	ניוטון	Eternal Law	חק עולם
Law of Gravity	חוק המשיכה	Law of the Universe	חק עולם

```
4/18:09  למש ח ה ו ל ב נ י כ ל חק ע ו ל מ זה יה יה ל כ מ כ ד ש ה   4/18:08
4/18:19  ח ק ע ו ל מ בר יתמ ל ח ע ו ל מ ה ו א ל פ נ י יה ו ה ל כ ו   4/18:30
4/18:30  ת א ל ה מ ב ה ר ימ כ מ א ת ח ל ב ו מ מ נ ו ו נ ח ש ב ל ל ו י   4/19:10
4/19:10  כ ב ס ה א ס פ א ת א פ ר ה פ ר ה א ת ב ג ד י ו ו ט מ א ע ד ה ע   4/19:20
4/19:20  ה ו א מ ת ו כ ה ה ק ה ל כ י א ת מ ק ד ש יה ו ה ט מ א מ י נ ד ה   4/20:10
4/20:10  מ ש מ ע ו ו נ א ה מ ר ימ ה מ נ ה ס ל ע ה זה נ ו צ י א ל כ מ מ   4/20:21
4/20:22  ש ר א ל ע ב ר ב ג ב ל ו ו יט י ש ר א ל מ ע ל י ו ו יס ע ו מ   4/21:05
4/21:05  ר ה ע מ ב א ל ה י מ ו ב מ ש ה ל מ ה ה ע ל י ת נ ו מ מ צ ר ימ
```

1

The cylinder size is 645. The table spans from Numbers 18:8 through Numbers 21:05.

FINDINGBYFABRICEBECT

This kind of table is a good example to illustrate the different kind of results that can occur with a change in protocol.

Using a standard protocol, we set the expected number of ELSs for each of the key words, including the snooped phrase to be 100.

With this protocol, the maximum skip searched for the key word: חוק, **Law** is 6 and thus the skip 12 ELS for חוקin the above table is never found.

In order to find a nearby ELS of the word חוק

With a sufficiently small skip, the table had to be row split, with a cylinder size of 325 and only the second ELS for חקעולם„Eternal Law'occurs in the new table which is shown next.

---

1.   http://torahcode.us/torah_codes/code_history/newton2.png

Newton	ניוטון	Eternal Law	חק עולם
Law of Gravity	חוק המשיכה		

4/18:19	בניכולבנתיכאתכל **חק ע ו ל מ** ברית מלחעולמהו	4/18:19
4/18:24	התרומהנתתיללויימלנחלהעלכנאמרתילהמבת	4/18:24
4/18:30	שוממנןואמרתאלהמבהרימכמאתחלבוממנוו **כ**	4/18:29
4/19:04	חטאתהלפניוולקחאלעזרהכהנמדמהבאצבעוו	4/19:03
4/19:10	תהואוכבסהאספאתאפרההפרהאתבגדיו **וטמא** עד	4/19:09
4/19:16	כלכליפתוחאשראינצמידפתילעליו **וטמא** האואי	4/19:15
4/19:20	**ה** ואמתו **כ** הקהלכיאתמק דשיה וה **טמא** מיונד **ה** לאז	4/19:20
4/20:05	ירנווולמהההעלית נוממצרימלהב יאאתנואלהמ	4/20:04
4/20:11	נאהמרימהמנהסלעהזה **ו** צ יאלכממימ ו יר מ מש	4/20:10
4/20:16	מ **ח** ולאבתינ וונצעקאליהוהויש מע **ק** לנ וו ישל	4/20:15
4/20:22	לוויטישראלמעל **י** ווי סעומק דשוי באוב ני יש	4/20:21
4/20:29	שמבראשההרווירדמשהואלעזרמנההרוירא וכל	4/20:28
4/21:05	**נ** וממצרימלמותבמדברכ יאי נלחמ ו	4/21:05

2

The cylindersize is 325. The table spans from Numbers18:19 through Numbers 21:05. With the expected number of ELSs set to 100, the probability that a text from the ELS random placement population would have as small a table area as the one produced by the Torah text is about 8.5/1,000.

When Rabbi Glazerson was looking at the last table, he noticed that if the table would be expanded a little, it would contain an ELS of the

This ELS is the minimal skip ELS in the Torah. The developed table is shown next.

Newton	ניוטון	Eternal Law	חק עולם
The Genius	הגאון	Law of Gravity	חוק המשיכה

```
4/18·19   וה נתת ילכ ולבנ יכ ולב נת יכאתכל חקע ולם בר יתמלחתע ולמ
4/18·24   יר ימ ול יה והתר ומה נתת ילל ו ימל נחלהעלכ נאמרת ילהמ
4/18·30   לב ואתמקדש ומ מ נ ו ואמרתאלהמבהר ימכמאתחלב וממ נ ו ן
4/19·04   למח נה ושחטאתה לפ נ י ו לקחאל ע זרהכה נמדמה באצבע ו וה
4/19·09   נ דהחטאתתה וא ו כ בסהאס פאתא אפרהפראהאתב גד י ו וטמא עד ה
4/19·14   ע ימ ים וכלכל יפת וחאשרא י נצמ ידפת ילעל י וטמאה וא וכלא
4/19·20   נפשהה ואמת וכ הקהלכ י אתמקדש יה והטמאמ י נ דה ילא זרק על
4/20·04   וב ע יר נ ו ולמהה על ית נ וממצר ימלהב יאאת נ ואלהמק ומהר
4/20·10   ע ו נאהמר ימהמ נהס לעה זה נ וצ יאלכמם ימ ו ירממשהאת יד ו
4/20·15   ימ ולאבת י נ ו ו נצעקאל יה וה ו ישמע קל נ ו ו יש לח מלאכ ו י צ
4/20·22   ל ו ו יט ישראלמעל י ו ו יס עו ומקדש י יבא וב י ישראלכלה עד
4/20·28   מ בראשהתהר ו ירדמשה ואל ע זרמ נהר ו יראוכלה עדהכ י ג ו ע
4/21·05   הה על ית ן וממצר ימלמ ותבמדברכ יא י נלחמ וא י נמ ים ו נפש
```

3

The cylinder size is 325. The table spans from Numbers 18:19 through Numbers 21:05.

FINDINGBYFABRICEBECTANDRABBIGLAZERSON

When Mr. Bect saw what Rabbi Glazerson added to the table, his intuition was inspired and remembering that Newton was a believer in G-d, he discovered an ELS of the key word:מאמין - Believer'.

The developed table is shown next.

Newton	ניוטון	Eternal Law	חק עולם
The Genius	הגאון	Law of Gravity	חוק המשיכה
Believer	מאמין		

```
4/18·19   וה נתת ילכ ולבנ יכ ולב נת יכאתכל חקע ולם בר יתמלחתע ולמ
4/18·24   יר ימ ול יה והתר ומה נתת ילל ו ימל נחלהעלכ נאמרת ילהמב
4/18·30   ן ו ר לב ואתמקדש ומ מ נ ו ואמרתאלהמבהר ימכמאתחל ב וממ נ ו
4/19·04   וה למח נה ושחטאתה לפ נ י ו לקחאל ע זרהכה נמדמה באצבע ו
4/19·09   נ דהחטאתתה וא ו כ בסהאס פאתא אפרהפראהאתב גד י ו וטמא עד ה
4/19·14   ע ימ ים וכלכל יפת וחאשרא י נצמ ידפת ילעל י וטמאה וא וכל
4/19·20   נפשהה ואמת וכ הקהלכ י אתמקדש יה והטמאמ י נ דה ילא זרק על
4/20·04   וב ע יר נ ו ולמהה על ית נ וממצר ימלהב יאאת נ ואלהמק ומהר
4/20·10   ע ו נאהמר ימהמ נהס לעה זה נ וצ יאלכמם ימ ו ירמשהאת יד ו
4/20·15   ימ ולאבת י נ ו ו נצעקאל יה וה ו ישמע קל נ ו ו יש לח מלאכ ו י צ
4/20·22   ל ו ו יט ישראלמעל י ו ו יס עו ומקדש י יבא וב י ישראלכלה עד
4/20·28   מ בראשהתהר ו ירדמשה ואל ע זרמ נהר ו יראוכלה עדהכ י ג ו ע
4/21·05   הה על ית ן וממצר ימלמ ותבמדברכ יא י נלחמ וא י נמ ים ו נפש
```

4

---

3. http://torahcode.us/torah_codes/code_history/newton3.png

The cylinder size is 325. The table spans from Numbers 18:19 through through Numbers 21:05.

David Bell has tables on his website: http://bellresearchlab.com/

Some of the tables are his own and some he has has obtained from other websites.

As mentioned initially, all these researchers use the Code Finder program's odd's ratio calculation or its inverse, the p-value probability, in evaluating their tables.

Unfortunately, the p-values calculated by the Code Finder program are not correct and do not correspond to the probability of any conceivable Torah code experiment.

It is not unusal for the score, that the Code Finder program producers to be three or four orders of magnitude too small.

'

---

[1]Newton would spend much of his life seeking and revealing what could be considered a Bible Code[5]. He placed a great deal of emphasis upon the interpretation of the Book of Revelation[6], writing generously upon this book and authoring several manuscripts detailing his interpretations. Unlike a prophet[7] in the true sense of the word, Newton relied upon existing Scripture to prophesy for him, believing his interpretations would set the record straight in the face of what he considered to be "so little understood". In 1754, 27 years after his death, Isaac Newton's treatise, *An Historical Account of Two Notable Corruptions of Scripture*[8] would be published, and though it does not argue any prophetic meaning, it does exemplify what Newton considered to be just one popular misunderstanding of Scripture.

Although Newton's approach to these studies could not be considered a scientific approach, he did write as if his findings were the result of evidence-based research.

[2]Professor Eliyahu Rips is an Israeli mathematician[9] of Latvian origin known for his research in geometric group theory[10]. He became known to the general public following his coauthoring a paper on what is popularly known as Bible code[11], the supposed coded messaging in the Hebrew text of the Torah[12]

---

4. http://torahcode.us/torah_codes/code_history/newton4.png

5. https://en.wikipedia.org/wiki/Bible_Code

6. https://en.wikipedia.org/wiki/Book_of_Revelation

7. https://en.wikipedia.org/wiki/Prophet

8. *https://en.wikipedia.org/wiki/An_Historical_Account_of_Two_Notable_Corruptions_of_Scripture*

9. https://en.wikipedia.org/wiki/Mathematics

10. https://en.wikipedia.org/wiki/Geometric_group_theory

11. https://en.wikipedia.org/wiki/Bible_code

12. https://en.wikipedia.org/wiki/Torah

[3]The Vilna Gaon was a Jewish Scholar, a Talmudist, Halakhist, Kabbalist and the foremost leader of misnagdic Jewry of the past few centuries. He is commonly referred to as 'The Pious Genius FromVilnius'Ha Gaon He Chasid Mi Vilna'.

[4]The Zohar is the foundational work in the literature of Jewish mystical thought known as Kabbalah.

[5]**Moses ben Jacob Cordovero** (Hebrew[13]: משה קורדוביר *Moshe Cordovero* ; 1522–1570) was a central figure in the historical development of Kabbalah[14], leader of a mystical school in 16th-century Safed[15], Ottoman Syria[16]. He is known by the acronym[17] the **Ramak** (Hebrew[18]: רמ"ק)

[6]It is the Glory of God to conceal a thing, but the honor of kings to search out a matter (Proverbs 25:2).

[7]**Exegesis** (/ˌɛksɪˈdʒiːsɪs/[19]; from the Greek[20] ἐξήγησις from ἐξηγεῖσθαι, "to lead out") is a critical explanation or interpretation[21] of a text, particularly a religious text[22]. Traditionally the term was used primarily for work with the Bible[23]; however, in modern usage *biblical exegesis* is used for greater specificity to distinguish it from any other broader critical text explanation.

Exegesis includes a wide range of critical disciplines: textual criticism[24] is the investigation into the history and origins of the text, but exegesis may include the study of the historical and cultural backgrounds of the author, text, and original audience. Other analyses include classification of the type of literary genres presented in the text and analysis of grammatical[25] and syntactical[26] features in the text itself.The terms exegesis and hermeneutics[27] have been used interchangeably.

[8] Halakha is the collective body of Jewish[28] religious laws[29] derived from the written[30] and Oral Torah[31]. Halakha is based on biblical commandments (*mitzvot*[32]), subsequent Talmudic[33] and rabbinic law[34], and the customs and traditions compiled in the many books such as the *Shulchan Aruch*[35]. *Halakha* is often translated as "Jewish Law", although a more literal translation might be "the way to behave" or "the way of walking". The word derives from the root[36] that means "to

---

13.   https://en.wikipedia.org/wiki/Hebrew_language

14.   https://en.wikipedia.org/wiki/Kabbalah

15.   https://en.wikipedia.org/wiki/Safed

16.   https://en.wikipedia.org/wiki/Ottoman_Syria

17.   https://en.wikipedia.org/wiki/Hebrew_acronyms

18.   https://en.wikipedia.org/wiki/Hebrew_language

19.   https://en.wikipedia.org/wiki/Help:IPA/English

20.   https://en.wikipedia.org/wiki/Ancient_Greek

21.   https://en.wikipedia.org/wiki/Interpretation_(logic)

22.   https://en.wikipedia.org/wiki/Religious_text

23.   https://en.wikipedia.org/wiki/Bible

24.   https://en.wikipedia.org/wiki/Textual_criticism

25.   https://en.wikipedia.org/wiki/Grammar

26.   https://en.wikipedia.org/wiki/Syntax

27.   https://en.wikipedia.org/wiki/Hermeneutics

28.   https://en.wikipedia.org/wiki/Judaism

29.   https://en.wikipedia.org/wiki/Religious_law

30.   https://en.wikipedia.org/wiki/Torah

31.   https://en.wikipedia.org/wiki/Oral_Torah

32.   *https://en.wikipedia.org/wiki/Mitzvah*

33.   https://en.wikipedia.org/wiki/Talmud

34.   https://en.wikipedia.org/wiki/Rabbinic_law

35.   *https://en.wikipedia.org/wiki/Shulchan_Aruch*

36.   https://en.wikipedia.org/wiki/Semitic_root

behave" (also "to go" or "to walk"). *Halakha* guides not only religious practices and beliefs, but also numerous aspects of day-to-day life.]37

[9]A kollel is an institute for full-time, advanced study of the Talmud and rabbinic literature.

[10]Gaon is a title given for a Jewish Scholar that is on a genius level of understanding and teaching.

[11]**Rabbi Auerbach** was a renowned Orthodox Jewish[38] rabbi[39], posek[40]- Scholar who determines the position of *Halakha*[41] – *Jewish Law*, and was rosh yeshiva[42] of the Kol Torah[43] Yeshiva in Jerusalem[44], Israel[45]. The Jerusalem neighborhood Ramat Shlomo[46] is named after Rabbi Auerbach.

[12]In its primary meaning, the Hebrew[47] word *mitzvah* (/ˈmɪtsvə/[48], meaning "commandment", מִצְוָה, [mitsˈva][49], Biblical[50]: *miṣwah*; plural מִצְווֹת *mitzvot* [mitsˈvot][51], Biblical: *miṣwoth*; from צִוָּה *ṣiwwah* "command") refers to precepts and commandments commanded by God, with the additional connotation of one's religious duty.

It is used in rabbinical Judaism[52] to refer to the 613 commandments[53] given in the Torah[54] at biblical Mount Sinai[55] and the seven rabbinic commandments[56] instituted later for a total of 620. The 613 commandments are divided into two categories: 365 negative commandments and 248 positive commandments. According to the Talmud[57], all moral laws[58] are, or are derived from, divine commandments[59]. The collection is part of the larger Jewish law or *halakha*[60].

[13]A **tractate** is a written work dealing formally and systematically with a subject; the word derives from the Latin *tractatus*, meaning treatise[61].

---

37.   https://en.wikipedia.org/wiki/Halakha#cite_note-2

38.   https://en.wikipedia.org/wiki/Orthodox_Judaism

39.   https://en.wikipedia.org/wiki/Rabbi

40.   https://en.wikipedia.org/wiki/Posek

41.   *https://en.wikipedia.org/wiki/Halakha*

42.   https://en.wikipedia.org/wiki/Rosh_yeshiva

43.   https://en.wikipedia.org/wiki/Kol_Torah

44.   https://en.wikipedia.org/wiki/Jerusalem

45.   https://en.wikipedia.org/wiki/Israel

46.   https://en.wikipedia.org/wiki/Ramat_Shlomo

47.   https://en.wikipedia.org/wiki/Hebrew_language

48.   https://en.wikipedia.org/wiki/Help:IPA/English

49.   https://en.wikipedia.org/wiki/Help:IPA/Hebrew

50.   https://en.wikipedia.org/wiki/Biblical_Hebrew

51.   https://en.wikipedia.org/wiki/Help:IPA/Hebrew

52.   https://en.wikipedia.org/wiki/Rabbinical_Judaism

53.   https://en.wikipedia.org/wiki/613_Mitzvot

54.   https://en.wikipedia.org/wiki/Torah

55.   https://en.wikipedia.org/wiki/Biblical_Mount_Sinai

56.   https://en.wikipedia.org/wiki/Mitzvah#Rabbinical_mitzvot

57.   https://en.wikipedia.org/wiki/Talmud

58.   https://en.wikipedia.org/wiki/Moral_code

59.   https://en.wikipedia.org/wiki/Divine_law

60.   *https://en.wikipedia.org/wiki/Halakha*

61.   https://en.wikipedia.org/wiki/Treatise

One example of its use is in citing a section of the Talmud[62], when the term *Masekhet*[63] (מסכת) is used in conjunction with the name of the subject, for example, MasekhetBerakhoth[64], which is relevant to agriculture and blessings.

[14]I.e.The written Torah says to the Jewish People, when a fish is found in the ocean, one needs to inspect it first for two anatomical features before it is consumed, which is to look for: Fins and scales. If it has these 'two witnesses' it is considered a kosher fish.

Comes the Oral Torah along and makes the following statement:

Every species that one is going to find in any body of water they search in, that fish that was found that has scales must <u>always</u> have fins, guaranteed, without any exception. How many types of fish do we know today? More than 40,000 different types of fish. That does not include scorpions, turtles and snakes and so many other types of animals that live in the ocean.Alone the types of fish known today to man are around 40,000 in number.

The Torah explains to us, if one picks up a fish and it has scales one must not worry, it will always have fins. Which means if one person ever in history found a fish that does have scales but no fins, this would constitute the end of the Torah. Never since the giving of the Torah was there a person finding such a fish and making such a claim. Like that G-d proves to man that the Torah can't be written by human hand. Because who can know all? Just the Creator of this world. This allows the wisdoms of the Torah to be glorified and honored in the eyes of man.

[15]In Judaism it is taught that the study of Torah is the only real meaningful way to uplift, arouse and give immense pleasure to the soul and also ease the plight of an afflicted soul. Akin as vital as water is to the body, Torah is as vital to the soul.

[16] What are the Seven Sciences referred to by the Gaon of Vilna? It is not easy to define them precisely, but they could be translated approximately as follows: 1) mathematics, astronomy, and geometry, 2) all types of composition and construction, 3) medicine, 4) grammar, 5) sacred music, 6) the science of perfecting and combining things, 7) psychology and the science of connecting the material to the spiritual.

[17] The *milui* is obtained by writing out the name of each letter in a word, and taking the numerical value of the names of the letters.

[18]*ShneiLuchotHabrit,* part 1, *MasechetPesachim* 8, on *Midrash Kohelet, Midrash Rabba* 11:8.

[19]**Moses ben Maimon** (Arabic[65]:), commonly known asموسى بن ميمون **Maimonides** (/maɪˈmɒnɪdiːz/[66] *my-MON-i-deez*[67]) and also referred to by the acronym **Rambam**, was a medieval Sephardic Jewish[68] philosopher[69] who became one of the most prolific and influential Torah[70] scholars of the Middle Ages[71]. In his time, he was also a preeminent astronomer[72] and physician. Born in Córdoba[73], Almoravid empire[74] (present-day Spain[75]) on Passover Eve[76], 1138, he worked as a rabbi, physician, and philosopher in Morocco[77] and Egypt[78].

---

62. https://en.wikipedia.org/wiki/Talmud

63. *https://en.wikipedia.org/wiki/Masekhet*

64. https://en.wikipedia.org/wiki/Berakhot_(Talmud)

65. https://en.wikipedia.org/wiki/Arabic_language

66. https://en.wikipedia.org/wiki/Help:IPA/English

67. *https://en.wikipedia.org/wiki/Help:Pronunciation_respelling_key*

68. https://en.wikipedia.org/wiki/Sephardi_Jews

69. https://en.wikipedia.org/wiki/Jewish_philosophy

70. https://en.wikipedia.org/wiki/Torah

71. https://en.wikipedia.org/wiki/Middle_Ages

72. https://en.wikipedia.org/wiki/Astronomer

73. https://en.wikipedia.org/wiki/C%C3%B3rdoba,_Spain

74. https://en.wikipedia.org/wiki/Almoravid_dynasty

75. https://en.wikipedia.org/wiki/Spain

76. https://en.wikipedia.org/wiki/Passover_Eve

[20]Thesatan is in the Jewish teachings not a fallen angel that wrestles with G-d about the ultimate power. He is rather an accuser (adversary) who is created by G-d and works for G-d to test mankind. Just as the verse says: 'I form the light, and create darkness: I make peace, and create evil: I the LORD do all these things (Isaiah 45:7). According to Jewish teachings the Satan and the angel of death is the same angel.

[21]There is a well-known and respected Jewish Tradition that there are 'Two Messiahs'. One being, 'Messiah Son of David', who is universally known as the Messiah King and who will reign mankind at the ultimate End. However, there is a lesser known or even hidden but well-respected tradition about a Messiah called 'Messiah Son of Joseph'. Who could also be called for demonstration purposes, 'The Messiah of The World of Action'? Messiah Son of Joseph is responsible for leading the Jewish people and mankind here on earth safely into the End Times.

At a certain point of this accomplishment reached, Messiah Son of David takes over and a messianic kingdom will be established with Messiah Son of David as the Messiah King and Messiah Son Of Joseph as the Viceroy.

A Jewish perspective of the 'Material World' which is also called the 'World of Action' and Heaven which is also called the 'World to Come:

The material world in Jewish Teachings is called 'The World of Action'. Why you might ask? Because only in this world can we grow as human beings, change our actions, exercise free will and effect and change our environment etc.... Once a person dies, he cannot bargain with G-d in the heavenly court. A human being might stand in the heavenly court and see and talk to G-d, but he will not be able to change anything.

He will only receive his reward or punishment in the precise manner of his actions on earth. Therefore, one could say that the Messiah Son of Joseph is the Messiah of the Material plane level, where he can cause change within us. The Messiah Son of David is more on the level of the ultimate reward and therefore enormous pleasure, like someone would derive by basking in the Light Of G-d as often reported for instance in Near Death Experiences. That said any effort even to the most minute degree of unlocking godliness in this world, contains a spark of that pleasure Of the Light Of G-d, a taste of the Afterlife/ The World To Come and the Redemption.

The goal is to intensify that pleasure, till its essence overwhelms all reality and all senses, breaking away all darkness in the material world. That said in the endless kindness and mercy of G-d there are ways to change a fixed decree of a deceased relative or teacher. Every good deed we do in their name such as prayer, tzedakah which means charity, or by saying the Mourning prayer, called 'Kaddish' for the deceased one, one can ease the plight and raise their soul in the World To Come. Yet the most that one can do is here in the World of Action. Therefore, one should take full advantage of his own life on earth.

77.   https://en.wikipedia.org/wiki/Morocco

78.   https://en.wikipedia.org/wiki/Egypt

[22]**Eleazar of Worms**[79] (אלעזר מוורמייזא) (c. 1176–1238), or **Eleazar ben Judah ben Kalonymus,** also sometimes known today as **Eleazar Rokeach** ("Eleazar the Perfumer" אלעזר רקח) from the title of his *Book of the Perfumer* (*Sefer ha rokeah* ספרהרקח)—where the numerical value[80] of "Perfumer" (in Hebrew[81]) is equal to Eleazar, was a leading Talmudist and Kabbalist[82], and the last major member of the *HasideiAshkenaz*[83], a group of German Jewish[84] pietists[85].

[23]*Me'amLo'ezt* (Hebrew[86]:), initiated by Rabbiזלועם מעם Yaakov Culi[87] in 1730, is a widely studied commentary[88] on the Tanakh[89] written in Ladino[90]. It is perhaps the best-known publication in that language.

[24]**Yosef Hayim** (1 September 1835 – 30 August 1909) (Iraqi Hebrew[91]: **YosephḤayyim**; Hebrew[92]: יוסף חיים was a leading Baghdadi (מבגדאד *hakham*[93] (Sephardi[94] rabbi[95]), authority[96] on *halakha*[97] (Jewish law), and Master Kabbalist[98]. He is best known as author of the work on *halakha*[99] ***Ben IshḤai*** (בן איש חי) ("Son of Man (who) Lives"), a collection of the laws of everyday life interspersed with mystical[100] insights and customs, addressed to the masses and arranged by the weekly Torah[101] portion.

[25]**Bahya ben Asher ibn Halawa** (בחיי בן אשר אבן חלואה, 1255–1340) was a rabbi[102] and scholar of Judaism[103]. He was a comme"""ntator on the Hebrew Bible[104]. He was one of two people now known as **RabbeinuBehaye**, the other being philosopher Bahya ibn Paquda[105].

---

79. https://en.wikipedia.org/wiki/Worms,_Germany

80. https://en.wikipedia.org/wiki/Gematria

81. https://en.wikipedia.org/wiki/Hebrew_language

82. https://en.wikipedia.org/wiki/Kabbalist

83. *https://en.wikipedia.org/wiki/Hasidei_Ashkenaz*

84. https://en.wikipedia.org/wiki/Jewish

85. https://en.wikipedia.org/wiki/Pietist

86. https://en.wikipedia.org/wiki/Hebrew_language

87. https://en.wikipedia.org/wiki/Yaakov_Culi

88. https://en.wikipedia.org/wiki/Exegesis

89. https://en.wikipedia.org/wiki/Tanakh

90. https://en.wikipedia.org/wiki/Ladino_language

91. https://en.wikipedia.org/wiki/Mizrahi_Hebrew

92. https://en.wikipedia.org/wiki/Hebrew_language

93. *https://en.wikipedia.org/wiki/Hakham*

94. https://en.wikipedia.org/wiki/Sephardic_Judaism

95. https://en.wikipedia.org/wiki/Rabbi

96. https://en.wikipedia.org/wiki/Posek

97. *https://en.wikipedia.org/wiki/Halakha*

98. https://en.wikipedia.org/wiki/Kabbalah

99. *https://en.wikipedia.org/wiki/Halakha*

100. https://en.wikipedia.org/wiki/Mysticism

101. https://en.wikipedia.org/wiki/Torah

102. https://en.wikipedia.org/wiki/Rabbi

103. https://en.wikipedia.org/wiki/Judaism

104. https://en.wikipedia.org/wiki/Tanakh

He is considered by Jewish scholars to be one of the most distinguished of the biblical exegetes[106] of Spain[107]. He was a pupil of Rabbi Shlomo ibn Aderet[108] (the *Rashba*). Unlike the latter, Bahya did not publish a Talmud commentary. In his biblical exegesis, Bahya took as his model Rabbi Moses ben Nahman (Nachmanides[109]) or *Ramban*, the teacher of Rabbi Shlomo ibn Aderet, who was the first major commentator to make extensive use of the Kabbalah[110] as a means of interpreting the Torah. He discharged with zeal the duties of a *darshan* ("preacher") in his native city of Zaragoza[111], sharing this position with several others.

[26]**Midrash** (/ˈmɪdrɑːʃ/[112]; Hebrew[113]: מִדְרָשׁ; pl. Hebrew[114]: מִדְרָשִׁים *midrashim*) is biblical[115] exegesis[116] by ancient Judaic[117] authorities, using a mode of interpretation prominent in the Talmud[118]. The word itself means "textual interpretation", "study".

105.   https://en.wikipedia.org/wiki/Bahya_ibn_Paquda

106.   https://en.wikipedia.org/wiki/Exegesis

107.   https://en.wikipedia.org/wiki/Spain

108.   https://en.wikipedia.org/wiki/Shlomo_ibn_Aderet

109.   https://en.wikipedia.org/wiki/Nachmanides

110.   https://en.wikipedia.org/wiki/Kabbalah

111.   https://en.wikipedia.org/wiki/Zaragoza

112.   https://en.wikipedia.org/wiki/Help:IPA/English

113.   https://en.wikipedia.org/wiki/Hebrew_language

114.   https://en.wikipedia.org/wiki/Hebrew_language

115.   https://en.wikipedia.org/wiki/Bible

116.   https://en.wikipedia.org/wiki/Exegesis

117.   https://en.wikipedia.org/wiki/Judaism

118.   https://en.wikipedia.org/wiki/Talmud